# BAD FRUIT

## THE RESULT OF ONCE SAVED ALWAYS SAVED

Timothy Williams

Printed in the United States of America

Packaged by WinePress Publishing, PO Box 428, Enumclaw, WA 98022.



Unless otherwise noted, all scriptures are taken from the Holy Bible, New International Version, Copyright © 1973, 1978, 1984 by the International Bible Society. Used by permission of Zondervan Publishing House. The "NIV" and "New International Version" trademarks are registered in the United States Patent and Trademark Office by International Bible Society.

Scripture references marked NASB are taken from the New American Standard Bible, © 1960, 1963, 1968, 1971, 1972, 1973, 1975, 1977 by The Lockman Foundation. Used by permission.

ISBN 1-57921-556-4
Library of Congress Catalog Card Number: 2003101483

Dedicated to all who desire heaven more than a comfortable pew.

They do not cry out to me from their hearts but wail upon their beds. They gather together for grain and new wine but turn away from me. (Hosea 7:14)

# Contents

# Foreword

So what would you say when presenting Christ to an unbeliever?" the pastor asked with a pious grin. An uneasy pause of silence filled the room as he glared at the two of us from across the table. We noticed a twinge of jest in his tone of voice. He was the pastor of a small church near our home which had invited us to join his youth group on one of those "life changing" trips to Mexico where almost everyone plans to "save" at least one person. Now, having been motioned into his office, we sat across from one another, knowing exactly why he asked us this direct question. He had requested that each person in the group write individual essays on the message of salvation and how we might fulfill the Great Commission.

"The purpose of the essays," he continued, "was to prepare you for the mission trip." He went on to explain his shock and surprise at *our* interpretations of the Scriptures pertaining to the salvation call. He unmistakably did not agree with the truth clearly laid out in Scriptures we shared in our papers, nor was he prepared to defend his own position on the subject.

After several minutes of small debate, turning to the two of us he said, "I think it would be best if you guys just kept your ideas to yourself and not share them with anyone during the trip."

We weren't at all surprised. However, we couldn't believe how watered down and mushy this man viewed his own salvation. *Did he place no value on what Christ really came to do and what He in turn commands we do? Did Christ not mean it when He said that the road to salvation was narrow?* As we presented these questions and more it became evident to us that this man, although a pastor, knew very little Scripture and had lost his soul to an "easy believism" style of doctrine. As a result his life and congregation had been completely corroded with the bad fruit of unconditional salvation.

After we thoroughly presented the fundamentals of costly salvation, we added that we could not do as he had requested. At that we were kicked off the team and out of the mission trip entirely. We had struck a nerve too painful for him to handle.

The pollutant of Once Saved Always Saved was much more potent and deadly than either of us had at first realized. It had robbed this small church of any fear of God. *Why?* We wondered. *Why was it so hard for them to understand when the Scriptures are more than clear on the subject?*

After losing the opportunity to travel to Mexico with that particular church, another invited us to join their mission team down to the same place. The attitude and atmosphere of this team seemed much different than the previous. Learning from our past experience, we joined this group fully aware of our possible doctrinal discrepancies, yet unaware of how common the doctrine of once saved always saved really was in most churches. Sharing the same view of salvation as the original group, this youth team actually took it to the next level. Not only was salvation guaranteed for all who had prayed "the prayer," but then they never expected it to be practiced in daily life. In other words, you could be a Christian and yet resemble nothing of Christ's character—the results of the bad fruit of the teaching of "once saved always saved." Because of their laid back attitude, this particular mission team did not even think it necessary to bring along Bibles or any other basic outreach materials to Mexico. (Our own dad, though not attending the trip, made a mad rush to purchase Spanish bibles for us to take with us.) Again we felt surprised and dumbfounded at the results of cheap grace. These youths, most of whom were older than us, had a very shallow understanding of their God and it showed.

The bad fruit of an eternal security doctrine became more than evident on the trip home. As we traveled the group discussed about the happenings of the week. As we listened we could not help but feel disgusted at how pointless the whole trip had turned out. While the other teens boasted of how they had saved and brought others to "know Christ," we gently pointed out how imaginary and fake their good deeds may have been. Needless to say this was met with mixed reactions. Some thought we were crazy; others felt hurt, while still others zealously defended themselves.

It was absolutely amazing to us how these young Christians thought they fully understood what had taken the disciples years to comprehend. *Had the salvation call been watered down this much?* we both thought. We felt shocked at how easy and simplistic these young people viewed Christ's call of salvation.

"What about counting the cost? What about Christ's command that we should pick up our cross and follow

Him?" These questions and more were completely foreign to these young people. The concept of working our salvation out with "fear and trembling," was unheard of. They seemed more lost than the people we had just left in poverty stricken Mexico.

As the ominous desert landscape rushed past the two church caravans it became apparent that the results of cheap grace, easy believism, once saved always saved, or any other way of putting it, were literally catastrophic. These kids had no idea of the depth of walking with the Lord they were missing out on. Our discussion continued as we drove across Arizona. Finally, at a pit stop we were asked to move to the other van since the first group no longer wanted to spend time with us. The sun cast its last shadow of the day on our hearts as we continued to drive on through the night. While most of the teens slept we picked up steam in our discussion with one of the youth leaders.

For the first time we began to truly realize how such doctrine can completely corrupt and poison the very foundation of what Christ came to live and preach. Taking just these two examples, we can see the results of compromise. An overwhelming flood of emotions filled our hearts as we came to realize this. We had been taught what was so clear to us as the truth, but had yet to fully realize what can happen when that truth is distorted. We understood where these teens were coming from and felt sorry for their misunderstanding of Scripture. We knew it wasn't really their fault but rather the parents, teachers, and pastors supposedly leading and guiding them in the ways of righteousness.

The plague of easy salvation springs from more than some misguided misconceptions of Scripture. The doctrine of once saved always saved denotes more than a different belief system introduced by Calvin and those like him. It is the bad fruit that poisons the very salvation call that Christ came to bring. All of us agree that Christ came to die for our sins but few can believe He would even dare to call us to do the same. Churches today view the basic and fundamental concepts of the gospel as legalism and if you even whisper the word "works," you run the risk of being labeled a heretic. The people that we accompanied to Mexico had never heard of a costly salvation and we can't blame them for defending their beliefs. Furthermore, none of them had been taught differently and so we understood their concerns. How sad to see how their church had fed each one of these young missionaries a salvation gospel so contrary to what the Bible teaches, and how they took delight in spreading the same compromising doctrine to those needing Christ in Mexico.

Anyone can find comfort in a wide road gospel. But few will walk the narrow road and even fewer will enter the gates of heaven. Those who now share the glory of heaven know what it took to get there and they have left behind them a guide that will forever cast a straight and unswerving line to those shining gates. We who now search for answers have only to find the map and then go wherever it may lead us, even if that means losing our very lives to obtain it. This gives power to Scripture, validity to prayer, and a clear understanding to God's most precious gift of salvation.

It is our prayer that as you read this book, you will allow the Holy Spirit to open your eyes to those areas in your life that are lax or compromising. Examine your heart and let the convicting waters of Truth wash you clean of any selfish twisting of Scripture that might fill your repertoire of beliefs. Please take a long look at the tree of your life and see if any bad fruit hangs on your branches. It is our hope that your mind and heart will also be opened to what Jesus says really saves a man. Allow the fear of God to penetrate your roots so that you might be a bearer of clean, fresh, and holy fruit for the kingdom. As you read this book allow the Holy Spirit to search your heart to see if you too have consumed the bad fruit.

—Joshua and Josiah Williams

# Chapter 1

# Jesus Spoke Clearly

He taught them many things by parables, and in his teaching said: (Mark 4:2)

The debate of whether someone can fall from God's grace has raged for decades. To find the truth in this matter, let us examine the parable of the sower, where Jesus used the words "believes" and "falls away" to show that some individuals could lose their salvation. If He used those very words, then that should end any debate. But, sadly, not even the words of Jesus Himself can silence those who believe in once saved always saved.

Jesus definitely declares that some individuals have faith in Him but fall away. A hundred page commentary is not needed on this issue. Jesus expressed himself with absolute clarity. The additional words of men are only clouds that shut out the clear sunlight.

In this parable, Jesus used the ground to represent the different types of hearts in men. Jesus moved from those who have hard hearts to those who have soft hearts. Jesus first talked about people with totally hard hearts. In such cases, Satan can snatch the Word away so that they do not believe the truth. Since faith comes from hearing the Word, these individuals cannot believe because Satan can remove the Word from them immediately.

> The farmer sows the word. Some people are like seed along the path, where the word is sown. As soon as they hear it, Satan comes and takes away the word that was sown in them. (Mark 4:14–15)

This applies to the vast majority of mankind. Their hearts remain so hard that they do not, and cannot, believe Jesus is the way to life. Preaching has little or no effect on them and, as such, they cannot be saved. As recorded in Luke, they cannot "believe and be saved."

> Those along the path are the ones who hear, and then the devil comes and takes away the word from their hearts, so that they may not believe and be saved. (Luke 8:12)

I once spent a day sharing the gospel with a man who literally told me the very next day, "I can't remember anything we talked about. What *did* we talk about?"

Jesus then spoke of those who, and I quote, "believe for a while" but later "fall away." We know such people are actual believers because Jesus said that they "hear the word and at once *receive* it with joy" (emphasis added). Paul confirms this in 1 Thessalonians 2:13 when he writes, "And we also thank God continually because, when you *received the word of God,* which you heard from us, you accepted it not as the word of men, but as it actually is, the word of God, which is at work in you who believe" (emphasis added). The "word of God" is doing its "work" in the person who believes on Jesus. Thus it is the work of God and not the works of man.

It is a saving faith because it is a belief in Jesus. They accept who Jesus is and what He came to do. We know this is true because they "received it with joy," the result of saving grace being poured into someone's life. We see this in the jailer who came to "believe" in God. He was "filled with joy" because of this belief.

> The jailer brought them into his house and set a meal before them; he was filled with joy because he had come to believe in God—he and his whole family. (Acts 16:34)

You might think that Jesus should have the final word on the topic but, unfortunately, this is not the case. Instead, men resort to all kinds of textual trickery and deceptive and hollow philosophies in an effort to make Scripture fit their own mold and ease their troubled souls. For it certainly feels troubling to contemplate that three-fourths of those touched by God's Word miss out on salvation. This is, however, part of the offensive message of the cross, and we either choose to accept God on His terms[1] or make Jesus into an idol of our own design.

## Fallen Believers

Again, Luke recorded Jesus as saying they "believe." They are believers in every sense of the word. Their hearts "receive" the living Word and their lives declare they are full of joy. The seed begins to grow, giving evidence of new life. Such people try to obey Scripture, something the unbelieving world never attempts to do. But, as Jesus said, they have no root. They do not allow the grace of the new life to penetrate deeply.[2] So, as Mark wrote, when "trouble or persecution comes because of the word," they "fall away."

Others, like seed sown on rocky places, hear the word and at once receive it with joy. But since they have no root, they last only a short time. When trouble or persecution comes because of the word, they quickly fall away. (Mark 4:16–17)

God thought it worthwhile to have Luke repeat the words of Jesus, and so we will do the same. Again, we find that Jesus said clearly, "in the time of testing they fall away."

Those on the rock are the ones who receive the word with joy when they hear it, but they have no root. They believe for a while, but in the time of testing they fall away. (Luke 8:13)

Jesus taught that these believers have true faith, but they simply do not persevere in it. There can be no question, therefore, that Jesus referred to people with a true and saving belief in Himself.

In answer to the straightforward question, "Is it possible for people to believe then fall away?" Luke 8:13 contains Jesus' defining answer. Yes, "in the time of testing they fall away." How much clearer could He have been? But, alas, our sinful flesh does not want to accept this.

## Thorny Christians

The next kind of person Jesus spoke of lasts longer than the previous kind, but not long enough to save them in the end. Such types of people fellowship with "thorns." We would call them "worldly Christians." They attend churches where the message of the cross is reduced to the story of the crucifixion. In other words, Jesus died for us 2000 years ago, and that is the extent of the gospel. The concept that a person must be crucified daily and always carry the death of Jesus in their lives has been lost.[3] Instead of having the cross which crucifies them to the world, "life's worries, riches, and pleasures" choke them and they never mature. We can see this in church bulletins and Christian magazines advertising only fun and entertainment rather than reflecting the holiness worked by the cross. Or perhaps they have come to worship their ministry more than God and so never mature in the message of the cross.

> The seed that fell among thorns stands for those who hear, but as they go on their way they are choked by life's worries, riches and pleasures, and they do not mature. (Luke 8:14)

> Still others, like seed sown among thorns, hear the word; but the worries of this life, the deceitfulness of wealth and the desires for other things come in and choke the word, making it unfruitful. (Mark 4:18–19)

Desires for the things of the world, the worries of living a nice comfortable Christian life, concerns about money, or just wanting to have a good time, keep these seeds from becoming mature or fruitful. They grow by taking in grace, mercy, and the Word, but they bear nothing of value for God. They merely enjoy the things of God for themselves, and so remain selfish at their very core. Like the five foolish virgins, even though they waited in faith for Jesus to return, they never got beyond a self-centered trust in God.

**Cut Off Branches**

Because such believers refuse to move on to maturity, God will cut them off. We will explore this concept more fully in another chapter. But, for now, note that Jesus declared that God cuts off every branch *in him* that does not bear fruit.

He cuts off every branch in me that bears no fruit, while every branch that does bear fruit he prunes so that it will be even more fruitful. (John 15:2)

Jesus did not say that these people will just lose some of their reward in heaven. He stated that they are completely cut off from the vine. And who is the vine? It is Jesus Christ Himself, as Jesus made clear in the previous verse. And God is the "gardener" who, as we will see, will not permit a man to return to Jesus once he or she falls away.

I am the true vine, and my Father is the gardener. (John 15:1)

These withering branches are "picked up, thrown into the fire, and burned." Not just their works, or their fruit, or their rewards are burned, but the branches themselves. For Jesus explained that they are burned because they *don't have* enough fruit or reward.[4] The "branch" itself is dry and dead, because it has been cut off from life giving nutrients and graces.

I am the vine; you are the branches. If a man remains in me and I in him, he will bear much fruit; apart from me you can do nothing. If anyone does not remain in me, he is like a branch that is thrown away and withers; such branches are picked up, thrown into the fire and burned. (John 15:5–6)

At first, these branches may not realize that they have been cut off from Christ. They slowly wither over time. No branch withers instantly when it is cut off from a tree or vine. Even if the branch starts to wither while still attached, it fools itself by thinking there is no danger. For this reason, Jesus often warned that we will "not know at what time I will come."

It takes time, and therefore many who have been cut off from Christ don't realize it until many years later. In fact, many go to their death bed with little clue they have been cut off, because they still see some green in a very dry life. They play the fool to the end, never testing themselves[5] to see if they are fully in Christ.

Most likely some people reading this book have already fallen away but don't realize it because they have a little sap still left. Let us not foolishly think that every man who falls away can be known by all the heinous sins he commits. For the vast majority, it will not become obvious that they have fallen from grace until years down the road. And, even then, they will not realize it, because they have slowly become accustomed to their dryness.[6] In fact, such people are so blind that they come to think of their sad state as the normal Christian life. Such is the condition of those who have fallen from the Light of the Holy Spirit. Though on the verge of being dead in Christ, they think themselves alive.[7] Just one of the bad fruits of eternal security we see today are the smug churches that are closed to the commands of God, unaware of all the ways they disobey.

When discussing this issue, most will readily admit and even declare that we can find Scriptures "on both sides" of the issue. While we know in our hearts this is not true, it does appear at times as if that were the case. The solution to this apparent dilemma is both simple and clear. We must turn to Jesus. From the mouth of Jesus all Scripture can be understood. The very lips of Jesus declared that a man can believe and then fall away. To use any other Scripture to fight against those words means to try and use God's Word to rebuke the Son of Man.

Do not add to his words, or he will rebuke you and prove you a liar. (Proverbs 30:6)

If you are called by God, you have a choice. You can choose to keep the righteousness of God in your life or choose to lose that righteousness and your salvation. Jesus made clear the fact that once He makes you salty—that is, full of His righteousness—if you lose that saltiness, God will throw you out to be trampled on by men. Indeed, as we will see, it is impossible—if you fall away—to be made salty again.

Blessed are you when people insult you, persecute you and falsely say all kinds of evil against you because of me. Rejoice and be glad, because great is your reward in heaven, for in the same way they persecuted the prophets who were before you. You are the salt of the earth. But if the salt loses its saltiness, how can it be made salty again? It is no longer good for anything, except to be thrown out and trampled by men. (Matthew 5:11–13)

# Chapter 2

# How Fruit Turns Bad

Wisdom is better than weapons of war, but one sinner destroys much good. (Ecclesiastes 9:18)

It smells sweet at first and then it stinks to high heaven. Such is the nature of apples when they first begin to rot and the nature of a doctrine called eternal security.

One bad apple can rot an entire basket of apples, just as one sinner destroys much good. Good fruit begins to rot after wounds inflicted by animals or processing machines allow fungi to eat away at the fruit. Likewise, one sin or false teaching can destroy all the good in a ministry. Take all the correct doctrines in a church or ministry, add false teaching and all the good will start to rot. The teaching that has probably caused the most damage in Christianity as a whole is eternal security. We now have the advantage of centuries of experience to examine the belief that once you are saved, you are always saved. The idea that, no matter what a person does or doesn't do, their salvation remains secure and their ticket to heaven punched. We will trace the sad state of the church today back to this error in doctrine. Throughout this book we will compare the effects of this doctrine to the results of bad fruit. As Jesus stated, "by their fruit you will recognize them" (Matthew 7:20). We too will recognize the bad fruit of once saved, always saved.

Once an apple receives a wound, fungi can begin to eat away at the fruit. There are two types of fungi that destroy an apple. The first one feeds off the apple while still allowing it to grow. Like this fungus, there are those who believe in eternal security, but still call for repentance in the church. Though their teaching appears beneficial and the church continues to grow, they only siphon off nutrients and life, since such a teaching never crucifies the sinful nature. Such people merely use the Scriptures to benefit themselves or their ministry.

Scientists call this biotrophic fungi. It feeds off the healthy fruit without actually destroying it outright. In comparison, similar individuals and churches stay content to live their comfortable Christian lives, going about their ministry work, without actively focusing on eternal security. But the rot remains and, with every new "apple" that appears, they begin to weaken the life that God tries to produce in others. Whether intentional or not, bad fruit is still produced within God's orchard.

Most apples, however, are destroyed by the second type of fungus which destroys every living cell in order to absorb the nutrients in the fruit. This exemplifies the way most churches spiritually die today. They offer no real call for repentance but remain satisfied with just claiming salvation for themselves. The vast majority of those who believe in once saved always saved fall into this category.

**Rotten Fruit**

Placing a rotten apple in a barrel will cause the whole barrel to decay over time. The rot is very contagious and sometimes inconspicuous. As the fungus eats the flesh of the apple, it creates a gas that weakens the other apples before the fungus even infects them directly. At first, the gas smells sweet, but as the gas increases the smell turns sour. So it is with the doctrine of eternal security.

At first, all the talk about once saved always saved "smells" sweet to the flesh, but later it produces weakened, if not dead, lives. Like a rotten apple in the bottom of the barrel, you don't even realize it's causing so much damage. Have you ever noticed how much a person who believes in once saved always saved talks? They participate in a great deal of talk, stories, debates, circular reasoning, and "what if" scenarios. This "gas" weakens obedience to Scripture and begins to injure those still young and healthy in the Lord. An advocate of once saved always saved has forgotten that the "kingdom of God is not a matter of talk, but of power."[1] They can spread their false hopes because they feel so secure, never realizing that their spiritual lives are rotting away.

**Crushing the Worm**

Jesus spoke of another major cause of apples going bad—a worm that never dies. The apple maggot or railroad worm, as it is often called, eats a tunnel into the apple and deposits its eggs. Certain apples remain so strong that they literally crush the worm as they continue to grow and no damage occurs. We can compare this to the type of person who crushes the false doctrine of eternal security by Holy Spirit inspired understanding of Scripture. If the worm dies before it can deposit its eggs, the damage to the apple is minimal. Likewise, if we crush this teaching before it lays hold of our hearts, it will never cause damage.

These worms can quickly ruin entire orchards if the trees stand close together. In the same way, the doctrine of once saved always saved can destroy whole groups and churches. Just as an orchard owner would never leave his trees unguarded against possible infection, so too the church must wake up and stand against a doctrine that has caused more damage than any cult or heresy in the history of the church.

Fresh apples have a sweet smell, but rotting apples contaminate and attract flies. Likewise the doctrine that teaches that a man's salvation remains secure no matter how much he sins, defiles the sweet perfume of the Lord's grace, mercy, and love. As we look around, after generations of doctrinal "gas" building up, we see that even the flies are beginning to die. The church today has so little fruit left that the multitude of flies cannot find anything worthwhile to feed upon. The folly of eternal security causes many good souls to be near the verge of Scriptural starvation. For all the good a church might boast of, the folly of once saved always saved outweighs it all.

> As dead flies give perfume a bad smell, so a little folly outweighs wisdom and honor. (Ecclesiastes 10:1)

## Protection of the Lord

The rough bark of an apple tree protects it from a hostile world and has a unique beauty for its designed purpose. This protection allows the life giving sap to move throughout the tree in order to produce the fruit. In the same way, the cross, a "roughness" from the Lord, allows the Holy Spirit to move in our lives so that we might bear fruit.[2] Defective or wounded bark cannot protect a tree.

Likewise, if a person's concept of the crucified live is wounded, they stand unprotected from their own flesh and from Satan. We must examine the offensive message of the cross just as an apple farmer inspects a tree's bark to insure its health. In addition, the farmer measures and tests the sap of the tree to see how healthy it is. We too must measure and test, but to merely test doctrine without testing the life makes one a Pharisee. On the other hand, to scrutinize a life and yet have a shallow understanding of doctrine makes a person a Sadducee, someone who doesn't really believe anything[3] and has no clue what it means to call on the name of the Lord.

> Watch your life and doctrine closely. Persevere in them, because if you do, you will save both yourself and your hearers. (1 Timothy 4:16)

A man's thoughts affect his life. What we choose to believe influences not only ourselves, but those who listen to us and witness our lives. Scripture tells us to watch our lives and doctrine closely, and Christians must examine both aspects by the power of the Holy Spirit. By testing *both,* we look at what Jesus called our "fruit."

In this book we will be looking at the teaching of once saved always saved, but we will also examine the fruit it produces in the lives of those who believe it. We will observe, by the power of the Holy Spirit, the life and doctrine of once saved always saved or eternal security.

In order to have correct doctrine and an acceptable life, we must first follow Jesus' command to "hate" our own life.

> The man who loves his life will lose it, while the man who hates his life in this world will keep it for eternal life. (John 12:25)

Even if a man's belief appears to agree with Scripture, he must "hate" that belief. The reason for this is simple. Our sinful flesh is incapable of agreeing with God, even when it seems as if it does. Jesus told us that our natural condition is so sinful and wretched that we cannot be in unity with God on anything. I might, for example, claim to believe with all my heart that Jesus is Lord. But, if I do this in the power of the flesh, it amounts to a big fat zero. Jesus put it this way:

> The Spirit gives life; the flesh counts for nothing. The words I have spoken to you are spirit and they are life. (John 6:63)

Think of the demon possessed girl in Acts 16:17. Though she shouted truthfully that Paul preached correctly about Jesus, she remained demon possessed, until Paul cast it out. Just as God does not require the confirmation of demons concerning His Son, He also does not need our flesh's agreement about correct doctrine. Indeed both demons and our flesh are actually liars trying to express truth—an impossible combination.

## Crucifying Doctrine

Men pick and choose which doctrines to believe in based on what their flesh likes. Some of those teachings may actually be true, but they are worthless if motivated by the flesh. As a result we find many churches with many different beliefs. Most men remain unwilling to hate their own opinions enough to allow God to work perfect unity in the church. We must therefore approach the doctrine of once saved always saved with a holy hatred of our own mind and flesh.

In my own flesh I would prefer once saved always saved to be true. Nothing would give my sinful flesh greater joy than to know that, no matter what I do, I will still be saved and go to heaven. People will always search for a church that makes them feel safe and cozy, and leaves their flesh intact. Men choose their own doctrines, rather than letting the words of Jesus kill their opinions and give them the mind of Christ. Instead of worshiping God by letting Him crucify our lives, we fashion an idol for ourselves and call it Jesus Christ.

No man can step outside of himself and see the Truth objectively. Only the cross, which has the power to crucify a man, can allow the Holy Spirit to show us the Truth. Where you find the message of the cross watered down or rejected, the power of enlightenment concerning Scripture will be absent. If you are unwilling to hate your own life, pick up a cross, and let Jesus lead you, this book will not make any difference. The depth of sin in man causes most to lock their heels in and refuse to accept the Truth, in spite of any and every evidence to the contrary. Just like the crowds yelling "Crucify him," men would rather crucify the Truth than give up their lies and false hopes. Only when we treasure the offensive message of the cross will we find freedom from this trap. Only a cross, that offends our doctrines and our life, can give us the eyes of Christ to see the Truth.

Satan can lead us down paths that end in our own injury. Our sinfulness causes us to falsely think we walk on the path of life, when we have really wandered off into the thorn bushes of compromise. If you choose to stop being a fool who delights in his own opinion, then an inexpressible joy awaits you. This same joy awaits all those willing to sacrifice their flesh-pleasing doctrine of eternal security and gain understanding by the cross of Jesus Christ.

A fool finds no pleasure in understanding but delights
in airing his own opinions. (Proverbs 18:2)

We would do well to examine ourselves to see if we are
rotten apples, or if we have worms tunneling through our
lives. We must humbly ask, just how much rot and fungi
has attached itself to our lives because of a foolish doctrine? As Paul told fellow Christians in Corinth—and don't
miss the subtle point here—as Paul told *Christians*, "examine yourselves to see whether you are in the faith."

Examine yourselves to see whether you are in the faith;
test yourselves. Do you not realize that Christ Jesus is in
you—unless, of course, you fail the test?
(2 Corinthians 13:5)

# Chapter 3

# True Salvation

But the seed on good soil stands for those with a noble and good heart, who hear the word, retain it, and by persevering produce a crop. (Luke 8:15)

The Scriptural definition of real "saving faith" looks very different from the way churches present it today. True faith does not resemble anything like the idea that, once you receive your ticket, you are guaranteed to arrive in heaven. Even in the world, anyone taking a trip will not arrive at his destination the minute his ticket is punched. He still must pack, dress properly, travel to the airport, get on the plane, and fly the distance. In the same way, a man does not enjoy the fullness of salvation as soon as he "asks Jesus into his heart." As we have already been told by Jesus himself, we must pass through the "time of testing." This persevering faith causes us to mature and bear fruit for Jesus. He will accept only this kind of fruit as faith that leads to full salvation. Jesus prayed that His disciples would bear "much fruit" and those that refuse to, He cuts off.[1]

People with this kind of faith have a "good heart, who hear the word, retain it, and by persevering produce a crop." Such perseverance lies behind the true meaning of the "Romans Road" verses, inevitably quoted by the wide-gate gospel preachers.

> That if you confess with your mouth, "Jesus is Lord," and believe in your heart that God raised him from the dead, you will be saved. For it is with your heart that you believe and are justified, and it is with your mouth that you confess and are saved. (Romans 10:9–10)

Confessing with our mouth that Jesus is Lord and believing in our hearts that God raised him from the dead is a lifelong process, not a one-step recipe for instant salvation. Neither the Lord, nor Paul, ever meant for Romans 10:9 to become a quick and easy formula that entitles anyone who simply mocks a "sinner's prayer" to go to heaven.

## The True Meaning of Romans 10

How do we know this? By the rest of Scripture! If there was ever a Scripture taken out of context on a galactic scale it is Romans 10:9. You will never find an example in the Bible of anyone being born again by reciting Romans 10:9, or by saying a simple "sinner's prayer."

Paul understood that a man's salvation requires perseverance. Therefore, in the same book of Romans, he wrote that we must remain in God's love. In fact, both Jesus and Paul use the same words; "cut off." Paul, in writing to the Romans, the very book used to justify a wide gate gospel call, reminds them that they reside in God's "kindness" at the moment, but they must "continue in his kindness" or they will be "cut off." Indeed, Paul told them to think about what they do not want to think about. To "consider" that they could be cut off.

> Consider therefore the kindness and sternness of God: sternness to those who fell, but kindness to you, provided that you continue in his kindness. Otherwise, you also will be cut off. (Romans 11:22)

In other words, not cut off from some heavenly reward, but separated from God's "kindness" itself. In fact, Paul boldly stated that, unless we share in the sufferings of Christ, we have no part in Him. Those who advocate once saved always saved must consider Paul a legalist, someone who preached salvation by works. For Paul stated clearly that unless we share in the sufferings of Christ, we will not share in His glory. He taught that we "are children" and "co-heirs with Christ," and I quote, "if indeed we share in his sufferings." We cannot expect to inherit eternal life if we remain unwilling to endure these sufferings.

> Now if we are children, then we are heirs—heirs of God and co-heirs with Christ, *if indeed* we share in his sufferings in order that we may also share in his glory. (Romans 8:17, emphasis added)

During these times of suffering, as we continue to confess His name, our faith bears fruit unto full salvation. This is the true meaning of Romans chapter ten. If, however, we disown Jesus and His words, He will disown us.

Paul's salvation experience sharply brings into focus the concept of calling on the name of the Lord throughout daily life. First comes the washing away of his sins, and then the "calling on his name." While Paul's baptism lasted only a moment, he would later call upon the name of the Lord during all of his tests, sufferings, and trials.[2]

> He stood beside me and said, "Brother Saul, receive your sight!" And at that very moment I was able to see him. Then he said: "The God of our fathers has chosen you to know his will and to see the Righteous One and to hear words from his mouth. You will be his witness to all men of what you have seen and heard. And now what are you waiting for? Get up, be baptized and wash your sins away, calling on his name." (Acts 22:13–16)

You can see why those who believe once saved always saved must accuse Paul of preaching salvation by works. Because Paul preaches that we must "endure" in order to "reign with Him," and if we do not do this He will "disown us." To disown means to reject that which one formerly owned.

> . . . if we endure, we will also reign with him. If we disown him, he will also disown us; (2 Timothy 2:12)

## Separated From God's Love

We can interpret this no other way than God cutting off His grace from man. If Jesus disowns a man, mercy and grace disown him. Therefore, Colossians declares that, once we have been "reconciled" to Christ, we must continue in faith. Otherwise, our faith up to that point will be in vain. This is an important "if" Paul wrote—"if you continue in your faith" you will be presented to Jesus holy in his sight.

> But now he has reconciled you by Christ's physical body through death to present you holy in his sight, without blemish and free from accusation—if you continue in

> your faith, established and firm, not moved from the
> hope held out in the gospel. This is the gospel that you
> heard and that has been proclaimed to every creature
> under heaven, and of which I, Paul, have become a ser-
> vant. (Colossians 1:22–23)

The bad fruit of the once saved always saved doctrine begins with the fact that it encourages a shallow understanding of salvation. This simple-minded concept of salvation teaches people to believe that nothing else matters other than saying a prayer and accepting Jesus into their hearts.

Those who preach once saved always saved foolishly convince themselves that the elect cannot choose to separate themselves from the love of God. While it is certainly true that no outside influence has the strength to separate the elect from God's love, we can bring this about ourselves by hardening our hearts or trampling on the grace and mercy of God. Therefore God tells us to make our "calling and election sure." To make something sure is to move forward from uncertainty to certainty. The Lord spoke this way through Peter because, consistent with the rest of Scripture, it is quite possible for the elect to "fall."

> Therefore, my brothers, be all the more eager to make
> your calling and election sure. For if you do these things,
> you will never fall, (2 Peter 1:10)

Once again, clinging to once saved always saved forces you to consider Peter a legalist who preached salvation by works. This can only be avoided by twisting what Peter wrote so much that his message becomes emptied of any real meaning and power. For Peter declared that if we "do these things" we will "never fall."

How do we know Peter was not simply talking about losing some heavenly rewards? Because, in the very next verse, Peter connects this belief with actually being welcomed into heaven, not receiving a reward from the throne of God. In short, Peter says a "rich welcome" not a "rich reward." Or, as the NASB puts it, "for in this way the entrance into the eternal kingdom of our Lord and Savior Jesus Christ will be abundantly supplied to you."

> . . . and you will receive a rich welcome into the eternal kingdom of our Lord and Savior Jesus Christ. (2 Peter 1:11)

Truly God can keep us from falling but the question arises—is a man willing to be kept? Are you willing to be prevented from falling by God's grace? Do you desire to always call on the name of the Lord, to confess with your mouth and believe in your heart, no matter what demands God places in your life? Before you say "Yes" you would do well to count the cost as Jesus instructed.[3] For God can indeed keep us from falling, but few hate their sin enough to want that "keeping" in their lives. Like Jesus who was enabled to go to the cross and suffer because He obeyed God, are you also willing to learn obedience from the sufferings of Christ in your life?

> To him who is able to keep you from falling and to present you before his glorious presence without fault and with great joy— (Jude 1:24)

God certainly can prevent us from falling, but we cannot selfishly use this Scripture to void any of the others we previously read. Likewise, if we choose not to continue in faith, we give God reason to cut us off.

**Twice Dead in Sin**

Jude warns us to contend against "twice dead" men in the church. Have you ever noticed how, when an apple rots, it develops brown spots? Compare this to the huge blind spots which let those who hate the Lord take up positions in the church. Believing in eternal security allows many dead preachers to stand in our pulpits today. Bad fruit always attracts flies.

Let me pause for a moment to mention the seriousness of this situation. Since those who believe once saved always saved do not believe a Christian can truly fall away, they cannot see that the church contains "twice dead" men. For them, this passage in Jude is meaningless. They can never contend against such men, because they do not believe they exist. Try motivating an army to fight a battle when the army does not believe the enemy is real. You will get nowhere fast. That army loses the battle before it even begins. Churches that teach once saved always saved are overrun with men "twice dead" because, instead of contending against them, they call them brothers! No wonder the church has turned into one big field of ruined apples. Whole orchards or denominations lay in rot because those believing in eternal security have zealously invited "rotten" men into their churches. Bad fruit finds a safe haven in such places.

What would you think of if you saw a fruit stand displaying a banner saying, "We don't believe there is such a thing as bad fruit?" Twice dead men simply don't exist in the minds of believers of once saved always saved, so no wonder such rotten fruit fills the pulpits, elder offices, ministry departments, and worship teams. With open arms, they embrace wicked men and women as full brothers and sisters, corrupting the very heart of the church.

Let us look at this Scripture more closely. A man can only be "twice dead" by first being born again. All of mankind experiences the first birth, coming into this world, and we are all born dead in sin. We are conceived in sin and sinners even in the womb.[4] Though physically alive and living, we are dead at birth. A man can only die twice in this world if he first receives a new life from God. In short, only those who have been born again have the possibility to be twice dead. If God grants a man new life and he falls away from that new life, he is dead again—twice dead. The book of Jude compares them to fruitless and uprooted trees, a clear similarity to Jesus' description of the fruitless branches that will be cut off.

> These men are blemishes at your love feasts, eating with you without the slightest qualm—shepherds who feed only themselves. They are clouds without rain, blown along by the wind; autumn trees, without fruit and uprooted—twice dead. (Jude 1:12)

## Time of Testing

The Book of Jude tells us that a man has no excuse for falling away. It teaches that God can give us the faith, obedience, and power to live the Christian life—but some people harden their hearts against the grace that saves them. Jude reminds us that the Israelites were a "delivered people," a saved people, but God "later destroyed" them. Think of it. They had enough faith to allow God to rescue them from Pharaoh and Egypt, a life of slavery and sin, but not enough to trust God in the desert. They professed faith but rejected God's commands, ways, and counsel.

Like so many in the church today, the Israelites could testify that God delivered them and even did great miracles in their lives, but they refused to pick up their cross daily.

The church should "already know all this" but it does not, because those who teach eternal security have blinded people to the true value of the blood of Jesus. We should understand that God saved the whole nation of Israel, yet many did not continue in this saving faith. They had enough faith to put blood around their doorposts (trusting in the blood of Jesus), they had enough faith to walk through the divided Red Sea (being baptized), but not enough faith to trust God in the desert (the crucified life). So God cut them off and "destroyed those who did not believe." Again, anyone who holds to once saved always saved must view Jude as a legalist who preaches salvation by works. After all, he quoted from the Old Testament and reminded the people that the Jews had to do something in order to be saved. They couldn't just ask God into their heart. They had to put blood on their houses, march through the Red Sea, and trust God in the desert.[5]

> Though you already know all this, I want to remind you that the Lord delivered his people out of Egypt, but later destroyed those who did not believe. (Jude 1:5)

The writer of Hebrews also knows that we must have a daily faith that confesses the name of the Lord in order to be saved. The writer of Hebrews put it this way.

> So, as the Holy Spirit says: "Today, if you hear his voice, do not harden your hearts as you did in the rebellion, during the time of testing in the desert." (Hebrews 3:7–8)

This is our time of "testing." Will you prove to have a full saving faith? It all depends on whether you hear the voice of the Holy Spirit moment by moment, and do not harden your heart against what He says to you. Yet another part of the bad fruit produced by the once saved always saved teaching is that it separates faith from obedience, when Scripture gives no separation. A man who has faith, obeys. Such a man obeys by faith, in faith, with faith, through faith—but he obeys God. For example, water baptism is not merely a proof of saving faith, but saving faith in action. So much so that Peter tells us that unless one can do away with the resurrection of Jesus, one cannot do away with water baptism.[6] Scripture tells us that, from first to last, everything about a Christian's life should come from faith.[7] The man who stops obeying God, stops having faith in God. It is that simple. We see this point in the next passage, where disobedience and unbelief are viewed as one and the same.

> And to whom did God swear that they would never enter his rest if not to those who *disobeyed?* So we see that they were not able to enter, because of their *unbelief.* (Hebrews 3:18–19, emphasis added)

## Faith Leads to Obedience

In the last part of that verse we see the words "unbelief" and "disobeyed" used on equal terms. They are the same thing to God. The book of Titus describes God's grace as the power to obey.[8] A man who will not obey God, by faith everyday, will eventually cut himself off from the faith that saved him. This, of course, is why James tells us that faith without works is "dead." James focused on this point and flatly tells us that, if faith has no deeds, it cannot save a man from hell.

> What good is it, my brothers, if a man claims to have faith but has no deeds? Can such faith save him? (James 2:14)

Paul preached that we could not separate faith from obedience. But those who adhere to once saved always saved have made such an unholy division between obedience and faith that one cannot even mention obedience today without cutting through a barrage of points and arguments. Anyone who even suggests that certain Scriptures should and must be obeyed, will be accused of teaching "salvation by works." But let us see exactly what Paul preached.

> Through him and for his name's sake, we received grace and apostleship to call people from among all the Gentiles to the obedience that comes from faith. (Romans 1:5)

Did you catch that? An "obedience that comes from faith." What are we to preach? We must proclaim the same thing Paul did, an "obedience that comes from faith." A true saving faith is an obedient faith, not one that recites one prayer and thinks that will take you straight to heaven.

## True Legalism

For example, a man who claims Jesus as Lord and Savior but refuses to be baptized[9] as a believer does not have a true faith. He attempts to get around this to establish a righteousness that God never set down. The most ironic thing about the once saved always saved movement is that it, in reality, puts salvation under the law. Followers of the teaching are the true legalists because they refuse to "submit to God's righteousness" and, instead, establish their own.

Every time a man invents some other way of showing faith in Jesus, he places himself back under the law. Those who teach that we must say a prayer in order to be saved have made the good news of Jesus into a legalistic, human-effort gospel call. Simply put, those who truly believe in Jesus submit to what He said. Those who do not, make up something to suit their own liking.

> Since they did not know the righteousness that comes from God and sought to establish their own, they did not submit to God's righteousness. Christ is the end of the law so that there may be righteousness for everyone who believes. (Romans 10:3–4)

We can clearly see the bad fruit resulting from such legalism. But true faith in Christ puts an end of man's law and the old Law which stood opposed to us. Man's efforts and schemes have come to an end. At least, for those who do not rely on man's way of getting saved and submit to what God established.

In the Scripture below we see the nature of God's grace. God rains down grace onto our hearts. If we receive that power and surrender to it in humility, it will produce a good crop. However, if we use that power for our own selfish ends, refusing to die to self, we will produce thorns and thistles. Those who produce thorns and thistles become "worthless" and "in danger of being cursed." The term "in danger" shows that for the moment God's mercy covers them but they face a real threat that they and their fruit will be cursed.

Once again, they don't just lose their reward, but salvation itself for they are cursed just as Satan is cursed. For this reason the writer of Hebrews stated, "we are confident of better things in your case—things that accompany salvation."

> Land that drinks in the rain often falling on it and that produces a crop useful to those for whom it is farmed receives the blessing of God. But land that produces thorns and thistles is worthless and is in danger of being cursed. In the end it will be burned. Even though we speak like this, dear friends, we are confident of better things in your case—things that accompany salvation. God is not un-

just; he will not forget your work and the love you have shown him as you have helped his people and continue to help them. We want each of you to show this same diligence to the very end, in order to make your hope sure. We do not want you to become lazy, but to imitate those who through faith and patience inherit what has been promised. (Hebrews 6:7–12)

As we have just read, we must show the "same diligence to the very end" in order to make one's hope of being saved "sure." After all, as Paul wrote, who "hopes for what he already has?" This reveals the silliness of once saved always saved. It requires people to act as if they have already safely arrived in heaven. It is like believing the curse in the Garden of Eden is gone, that we have been totally saved now. That our gardens will not produce weeds, women no longer have pain in childbirth and men do not have to work for a living. This is the foolishness of thought that eternal security has produced. It has made wide the door for prosperity teachers and other false teachers to flood the church.

Ironically, those who believe in a once saved always saved doctrine actually have no hope, because they think they have already received as much salvation as possible. Yet Paul wrote, "in this hope we were saved." The hope that I *will be* saved works a certainty that I *am* saved. A man, however, already convinced that he is fully saved has no hope of salvation. He cannot hope for anything more than what he thinks he already possesses. A man must be sure of what he does not have to make sure he does not lose what he has been given.

For in this hope we were saved. But hope that is seen is no hope at all. Who hopes for what he already has? (Romans 8:24)

## Accepting God's Grace

God works it this way so that the hope of salvation might drive us to purity. But God does not play games. A man can lose his hope of salvation if he does not accept the grace of God in a worthy manner. Even in the world, if I give a gift to someone and tell them to wait until the appointed day to fully open it, they must guard that gift. If instead, they begin to abuse, mistreat, or ignore the gift, it would be taken back, and rightly so.

Similarly, the gift of forgiveness was taken away from the unmerciful servant and all of his sins reinstated. Consider the parable well. The man had been forgiven of all, his debt of sin cancelled. But by his actions, lack of obedience, God reinstated his debt of sin.

> When the other servants saw what had happened, they were greatly distressed and went and told their master everything that had happened. Then the master called the servant in. "You wicked servant," he said, "I canceled all that debt of yours because you begged me to. Shouldn't you have had mercy on your fellow servant just as I had on you?" In anger his master turned him over to the jailers to be tortured, until he should pay back all he owed. This is how my heavenly Father will treat each of you unless you forgive your brother from your heart. (Matthew 18:31–35)

Many may whine that this seems unfair. But God's ways are not unfair, rather it is our lack of appreciation for His mercy. This eternal security whine goes back as far as the Old Testament, when the Israelites complained to God about the same thing. Ezekiel preached the same message of repentance that Jesus preached, and the consequences of ignoring or watering down that message remain the same.[10]

The vast difference is that because of Jesus a man is completely without excuse, because grace could have empowered him unto righteousness. The point Jesus made in the parable on the previous page is even more clearly made in the Scripture below.

> But if a righteous man turns from his righteousness and commits sin and does the same detestable things the wicked man does, will he live? None of the righteous things he has done will be remembered. Because of the unfaithfulness he is guilty of and because of the sins he has committed, he will die. Yet you say, "The way of the Lord is not just." Hear, O house of Israel: Is my way unjust? Is it not your ways that are unjust? If a righteous man turns from his righteousness and commits sin, he will die for it; because of the sin he has committed he will die. But if a wicked man turns away from the wickedness he has committed and does what is just and right, he will save his life. Because he considers all the offenses he has committed and turns away from them, he will surely live; he will not die. Yet the house of Israel says, "The way of the Lord is not just." Are my ways unjust, O house of Israel? Is it not your ways that are unjust? Therefore, O house of Israel, I will judge you, each one according to his ways, declares the Sovereign Lord. Repent! Turn away from all your offenses; then sin will not be your downfall." (Ezekiel 18:24–30)

Likewise Paul encouraged Timothy to guard the gift with the "help of the Holy Spirit." But why guard something if there is no danger of losing it?

> Guard the good deposit that was entrusted to you—guard it with the help of the Holy Spirit who lives in us. (2 Timothy 1:14)

In order to be saved, a man must live as if he hopes for salvation. He must show zeal and diligence mixed with a good measure of fear and trembling. He must persevere in faith through trials and daily endure the offense of the cross. If a person "shrinks back" from this offense then God will be displeased and "destroy" that man or woman.

> But my righteous one will live by faith. And if he shrinks back, I will not be pleased with him. But we are not of those who shrink back and are destroyed, but of those who believe and are saved. (Hebrews 10:38–39)

Only those who continue in faith, hungering and thirsting for righteousness, will believe and be saved. All others who continue in their own self-assurance will be "destroyed," for God will never tolerate such self-righteousness. This bad fruit of eternal security causes individuals to remain unguarded against the fungi and worms that attack the good fruit God wants to work. Indeed, they feel little need to bear fruit at all, because salvation is all that matters. It is always amazing to listen to someone who believes in eternal security. They cry the loudest that people should bear good fruit, but their own lives demonstrate clearly that they feel self-satisfied with their religious condition. The fungus of hypocrisy and the worm of self-righteous pride infest their lives, killing the good fruit.

Chapter 4

# Falling Away

The master of that servant will come on a day when he does not expect him and at an hour he is not aware of. He will cut him to pieces and assign him a place with the unbelievers. (Luke 12:46)

How does one fall away and when does it happen? No man knows the exact point, but it definitely occurs. Indeed, those about to be cut off from Christ seldom are aware of the hour that Jesus assigns them a place with "unbelievers." For, as the Scripture above reveals, such believers are caught by surprise; another "blind spot" created by those who believe in eternal security. They cannot read the Son's face that can flare at any moment.[1] The first church rejoiced in this holy fear, but those who do not believe they can lose their salvation cannot receive it by grace.[2]

Only the Holy Spirit can make clear when someone falls away. And the Holy Spirit does speak this wisdom to disciples willing to listen. There have been times when God clearly told me that someone fell away. Not to pray for or ever hope again that they might be saved. While at other times God told me it was none of my business and, in most situations, I just don't have a clue. Often the heart of the person in question reveals the truth. Since repentance is a grace given by God, they cannot repent by grace when confronted with sin, a sure sign of being cut off from God. Of course, by repentance we do not mean the shallow, worldly sorrow over sin that is in the church, but true godly sorrow that comes only by the gift of grace.[3]

## Matters of the Heart

A man may fall away over something as obvious as murder, or as simple as a meal not eaten in God's will.[4] Of course, men can be forgiven for these things, but the determining factor is the heart. While most people in the church will boast that God knows their hearts and He knows they love Him, they forget that the heart is deceitful above all things.[5] A deceitful heart, filled with a doctrine of unconditional assurance of salvation, is actually ripe for damnation. The teacher of eternal security offers a doctrine that allows a deceitful heart to justify itself.

A man may fall away by committing sexual immorality or by having a bitter root in the church.[6] Any number of reasons can cause a man to miss the grace of God. As we read the Scripture below, note again that we can "miss" the grace of God. If a man does not seek "holiness," he cannot "see the Lord." In other words, he will not just miss a piece of his prize, but grace itself. For this reason, we must make "every effort" and to "see to it" that no one misses the Lord in the church. Like a ball and chain, eternal security slows down any real effort to move forward into the grace of God and Scripture. For to "make every effort" brings on every criticism by those who idolize once saved always saved.

Make every effort to live in peace with all men and to be holy; without holiness no one will see the Lord. See to it that no one misses the grace of God and that no bitter root grows up to cause trouble and defile many. (Hebrews 12:14–15)

It is a matter of the heart, not a matter of the Law. For example, take the difference between King Saul and King David. David committed far more obvious sins than Saul. And, on the surface of things, it seems that God rejected Saul over just a minor offense. But Saul's heart was bad. He was not "a man after God's own heart" like David. He would never let grace have its way. David was born as much of a sinner as Saul, but he allowed the grace of God to do its work. David permitted God to make and keep his heart soft. For this reason, Proverbs tells us to guard our hearts "above all else." But if a man cannot fall there is little motivation to guard a heart

Above all else, guard your heart, for it is the wellspring of life. (Proverbs 4:23)

**The Voice of the Lord**
A man begins to fall away when he gets out of step with the Holy Spirit and hardens his heart to the voice of God. Therefore the Bible tells us to "keep in step with the Spirit."[7] As he keeps moving further and further away, the Holy Spirit must "shout" louder and louder. Eventually, if the person does not repent and surrender daily, the Holy Spirit simply stops speaking. In due time, God will cut such branches from the vine. Like the fungus that feeds off the nutrients without actually destroying the apple, so too these individuals enjoy being connected to the vine even while they refuse to produce fruit. Simply put, God will not allow such

selfish believers to remain on the vine. He demands selfless fruit.[8]

Essentially, a man falls away by refusing to listen to and obey the voice of God. After all, salvation is not a matter of obeying a set of instructions laid out in Scripture. This is about active, daily fellowship, and hearing the voice of the living God—a voice that upholds all of Scripture but reaches beyond mere ink on paper. Many people talk of "having a personal relationship" with God, but live a delusion. Indeed, many people cannot really fall away, because they have nothing to fall away from except their Bible study or church doctrines. In order to truly fall away, a person must first have something to fall away from.

Such deliberate refusal to obey the voice of the Lord places us in grave danger of falling away. By God's grace He calls us to say "No"[9] to our own will and our own sin but, instead, we say "No" to Him. This rebellion leads to a hardened heart and a corrupted conscience and, if no repentance occurs, there will come a time when "no sacrifice for sins is left." It doesn't matter if the issue is over a television show or a ten dollar bill or the length of a person's hair.[10] When we say "No" to the Lord we place ourselves on a very slippery slope.

It is not true, that no matter what we do, God will always forgive. The man who is in Christ, who tramples, mistreats or insults the grace of God will not be forgiven. A Christian who is one of God's people will be judged by the Lord for such actions and attitudes of the heart. They cannot look forward to forgiveness, indeed, "only a fearful expectation of judgment and raging fire."

> If we deliberately keep on sinning after we have received the knowledge of the truth, no sacrifice for sins is left, but only a fearful expectation of judgment and of raging fire that will consume the enemies of God. Anyone who

rejected the Law of Moses died without mercy on the testimony of two or three witnesses. How much more severely do you think a man deserves to be punished who has trampled the Son of God under foot, who has treated as an unholy thing the blood of the covenant that sanctified him, and who has insulted the Spirit of grace? For we know him who said, "It is mine to avenge; I will repay," and again, "The Lord will judge his people." It is a dreadful thing to fall into the hands of the living God. (Hebrews 10:26–31)

If we "deliberately keep on sinning," even with our righteous sounding excuses like avoiding legalism or opposing salvation by works, there remains "no sacrifice for sins." If a man has "received the knowledge of the truth" and persists in disobeying the commands and ways of God, then only a "fearful expectation of judgment and of raging fire" will occur. Again, it is not works or rewards that burn, but the person himself. Every time someone responds lukewarmly to a command in Scripture or a demand for purity, they "insult the spirit of grace." For grace gives us the power to obey.[11] Far from exalting God's grace, eternal security tramples under foot the true grace and mercy of God. It dilutes the saltiness of God and makes dim the righteous demands of the Light of Jesus. Grace is presented only as unmerited favor that allows one to justify the wallowing in their sin. The bumper sticker "Christians aren't perfect just forgiven" reflects this whitewash approach to God's grace. A true bumper sticker would reflect what Paul wrote in the Bible, "Christians aren't perfect, but they are aiming for it. Correct me if you see anything wrong." After all, Romans is clear. Since we are not under law sin shall not be our master—we should be overcoming sin everyday.[12]

Undoubtedly the writer of Hebrews addressed Christians, because only true believers are "sanctified." Indeed, the word "sanctified" means to set apart for a holy purpose. A sanctified man has been freed from sin, in other words, born again. In John's words, "No one who is born of God will continue to sin, because God's seed remains in him; he cannot go on sinning, because he has been born of God."[13] But when a man deliberately ignores God and refuses to obey Scriptures, he chokes the new life and begins to fall away. Quite simply, the doctrine of once saved always saved is a license to ignore Scripture and is responsible for the falling away of millions.

**Stumbling or Falling?**

So, again, how can you tell when someone has fallen away? You can't, unless the Holy Spirit reveals it. And the Holy Spirit will reveal this to you only if needed. After all, you need to know who to pray for and who not to pray for.[14] We can never judge by outward appearances,[15] because we do not know what God will work in a person's life.

For one thing, there is a big difference between falling away and merely stumbling as one walks down the narrow road. There is a difference between wandering from the faith and falling from grace. Indeed, at times we can say a certain person has fallen from grace, and yet they still have a slight chance to return. We will explore that more in a later chapter.

A person can stumble yet not fall from grace. Of course, those who reject the idea of falling from grace often take things to extremes in an attempt to make their own position look better. They will object by saying that, if it is true that a person can fall from grace, then anyone who sins will lose their salvation instantly. They love to deliberately confuse stumbling with falling, but, in doing so, they miss the whole point. For, as the following passage reveals:

We all stumble in many ways. (James 3:2a)

If a man will humble himself, walk in the Light, and confess his stumbling, the Lord will delight in that man and keep him from falling away. But the man who self-righteously ignores his stumbling, claiming eternal salvation but refusing to confess his sins to God and man,[16] will be allowed to fall. For God does not delight in such a man.

If the Lord delights in a man's way, he makes his steps firm; though he stumble, he will not fall, for the Lord upholds him with his hand. (Psalms 37:23–24)

At times individuals will wander from the faith, much like when Peter denied Jesus three times. Actually, we must be very careful here, because Scripture does not say they wandered from the faith, but from the *truth*. Jesus told Peter he would deny Him three times. Peter denied the truth rather than accepting what he didn't want to believe. Had Peter accepted what Jesus said about him, he would never have stumbled. Many of those who believe in eternal security have had to learn some lessons the hard way because pride always goes before a fall. And eternal security breeds pride and deafens a man to the warnings given by Jesus through the Holy Spirit. What joy could be theirs if they could just humble themselves and say, "Yes, Lord, what you say in the Bible and about my life is true."

Remember, when Jesus predicted that Peter would deny Him, Jesus said, "But I have prayed for you, Simon, that your faith may not fail." Some men may wander from the truth to believe in once saved always saved, yet their faith may remain intact. Such men have not fallen away but have simply wandered from the truth, and can therefore repent. However, if over time they harden themselves to the calling to return to the truth about the Bible and themselves, they place themselves in very real danger of completely falling away.

> My brothers, if one of you should wander from the truth and someone should bring him back, remember this: Whoever turns a sinner from the error of his way will save him from death and cover over a multitude of sins. (James 5:19–20)

## Alienated from Christ

Finally, we see Paul telling the Galatians that they have fallen from grace. Indeed, he does not mix words here. In the clearest of language he proclaims that they "have been alienated from Christ" and have "fallen away from grace."

> You who are trying to be justified by law have been alienated from Christ; you have fallen away from grace. (Galatians 5:4)

In order to be alienated from someone, you have to first know them. The dictionary defines it this way; "to make unfriendly, hostile, or indifferent where attachment formerly existed." Where once Jesus embraced a disciple with deep attachment, that relationship is broken and replaced with hostility and indifference. If a person has been cut off, you can often see it in their eyes. The fire of the gospel is gone, they grope for any enlightenment or even conviction, hoping against hope that God will talk to them once again. Their wounded souls will even invent conviction and conjure up the voice of God in order to try and fill the void they now feel. It is incredibly sad to observe someone who has fallen away.

We can fall away by simply choosing to leave the Lord. God will never force Himself upon us. To do so violates love which never forces someone to love in return. Indeed, for God to force any man or woman to love Him is to turn them into robots. In John 6:66, and I trust the reader will note the number, we read that "many" made the choice to turn their backs on Jesus. Many people like this who, for reasons of doctrine or loving something in this world or even love of themselves, simply stop following Jesus.

> From this time many of his disciples turned back and no longer followed him. (John 6:66)

These people were not unbelievers and pagans. These were full blown, cross carrying "disciples," what Jesus told every church to go and make.[17]

So there are two ways to fall away. One, by hardening your heart against the "little" promptings of the Holy Spirit and, two, by simply choosing to stop following Jesus. In the first, God has to cut you off and, in the second, you cut yourself off by your own choice. The disciples in the above Scripture were offended by the tone, manner, and demands that Jesus made clear to them, and therefore hardened themselves against the gift of faith. These were *disciples* who, though they walked with Jesus, would not allow grace to have its way. We know that God did not choose to punish them without giving them a chance. God does not want anyone to perish and we understand that no man is predestined for hell. Indeed, if God has His will in the matter, if He were to force the situation according to His will, all would go to heaven.[18] Although, Jesus knows who will believe in

Him, He still turns to His remaining disciples to draw out
the grace of faith He works lest they ignore it and fall.[19]

> "You do not want to leave too, do you?" Jesus asked the
> Twelve. (John 6:67)

So it is with you. You have a choice. You can choose to
fall away and to leave. Do you want to leave now that you
know how tough the Christian walk is?

# Chapter 5

# Living Like This

Let us fix our eyes on Jesus, the author and perfecter of our faith, who for the joy set before him endured the cross, scorning its shame, and sat down at the right hand of the throne of God. (Hebrews 12:2)

How can you live your life like that? Thinking that if you fail to obey at any moment you might lose your salvation?" People will often ask me this question, and the answer is simple. I do what Jesus told me to do. I fix my eyes on Him who gives me grace and scorn the "shame" of the cross. In other words, I do not allow the suffering and humiliation of the cross to keep me from living this out. Instead of resorting to a comfortable once saved always saved doctrine that removes the offense of the cross, I rejoice in it and embrace its power to crucify me. After all, I have hope that I will be saved. And because I have this hope, I "purify myself" and therefore I am saved.

Paul declares this true when he speaks in Romans 8:24–25, "For in this hope we were saved. But hope that is seen is no hope at all. Who hopes for what he already has? But if we hope for what we do not yet have, we wait for it patiently." The most ironic thing about this is that, when a man hopes he will be saved, it is as if he "were saved." And the saddest thing of all is that those who believe in eternal security have no hope of being saved. They have received their "salvation" and thus have no reason to "wait for it patiently." As a result, the classic opening for the wide gate gospel call often goes like this; "If you died right now, are you sure you would go to heaven?"

In other words, their transformation by the saving grace of God never grows any greater than it is when they were first "saved." In presumptuous self-righteousness, eternal salvationists believe they will always remain in Christ. But for those that know they have been saved, are being saved, and will be saved, transformation becomes an ongoing process.[1] Indeed, they do not fully know what they will be in Christ.[2] Therefore, those who have this hope "purify themselves." They want to press onto the prize[3] of full salvation and transformation of becoming like Christ. Someone who holds to once saved always saved has no such hope, for they deny the need for hope in salvation.

Most people cannot even comprehend this concept. They think it must be terrible not to believe in eternal security. After all, how can anyone live like this? How can they live with such fear and trembling? How can a person endure all the soul searching and the offense of the cross? How can they accept all the humbling and pain God works in their life, fearing that they could lose their salvation if they say no to the leading of His voice? The answer is simple—because of the joy! A happiness and contentment so profound that I would never trade it for a mere façade called once saved always saved. God's way brings peace, and working out our salvation with fear and trembling should be every disciple's joy.[4]

## The Good News

In fact, the most unhappy people in the church today are those who believe in once saved always saved. What a heavy load of defensiveness and justification they carry around. It takes a lot of self-righteousness, and a lot of effort, to argue against God's Word every day and keep convincing themselves that this doctrine is true.

Those of us who have entered God's rest can easily see their pain and suffering. How sad, for it is easier to obey God than to kick against the goads.[5] They would find real peace if they just said "Yes" to the Lord instead of wearing themselves out arguing the points of eternal security. Another bad fruit of this doctrine is that it robs so many of true peace in the Lord, all in the pretense of trusting God.[6] What a bizarre illusion.

As I do radio show interviews, hosts often ask, "Don't you talk about the positive things of the gospel?" I'm always astounded by such a question. It only goes to show the poor state of the church. The cross *is* the good news. As Paul declares, it is the "power of God." Most Christians do not see this as "positive" because we don't understand it and refuse to have real faith. We want to keep our sin and our "self," and so we harden ourselves against the good news. Nothing else explains such reactions except that they are thieves trying to get into heaven some other way.[7]

After all, why can't people set aside the discussion about eternal security and simply discuss how to obey all of Scripture? What is better? To discuss the concept of eternal security, or to actually obey all that God commands us to do by the power of the Holy Spirit? Often, in debates with those who believe in eternal security, I will ask them, "OK, how then do I obey the Scripture in question?" They always refuse to discuss the practicalities because it is obedience they are trying to avoid. They are using eternal security as a smoke screen to avoid giving loving obedience to God. They would rather stick to the empty philosophy of eternal security. They forget Jesus told us to teach that all men should obey everything. Indeed, the great commission is obedience.[8]

At this very moment God convicts me of sin, reminding me of the day of judgment when I must bow before Him to give an account, of the seriousness of sin, and the slowness of my heart to obey His leading. But I am also filled by His Holy Spirit with "an inexpressible and glorious joy."

> Though you have not seen him, you love him; and even though you do not see him now, you believe in him and are filled with an inexpressible and glorious joy, for you are receiving the goal of your faith, the salvation of your souls. (1 Peter 1:8–9)

I have a "goal," the "salvation of my soul." Unlike those who believe once saved always saved, I refuse to sit still. I am in the process of "receiving the goal of my faith." For those who accept this it is not a matter of theological debate or dry dialogue, but of pure joy. Supreme joy! A joy the world and the worldly know nothing about. I know what it means to always, always, carry in my body the death of Jesus, so that I might have His life. So why would I ever trade this joy for the selfish lie of once saved always saved?

> We always carry around in our body the death of Jesus, so that the life of Jesus may also be revealed in our body. (2 Corinthians 4:10)

The race is not over, the test has not ended, and I have not passed through heaven's gate. Great dangers lie on the outside and on the inside. Every conviction of sin, every hardship, every rebuke, and every denial of self that God lays before me, I count as an inexpressible joy. And if, by grace, my heart remains soft, mercy will uphold me as I stumble along the way. What joy is mine while, with fear and trembling, I seek to "attain" that which I do not yet have, "the resurrection from the dead." How sad it is for those who have accepted once saved always saved, for they have no need to seek or attain anything. They are like runners sitting on the sidelines celebrating their victory before even running the race. Unlike Paul, who in the passage below speaks of sharing in the sufferings of Christ "so, somehow, to attain the resurrection from the dead." For Paul it was no sure thing he would go to heaven.

> I want to know Christ and the power of his resurrection and the fellowship of sharing in his sufferings, becoming like him in his death, and so, somehow, to attain to the resurrection from the dead. (Philippians 3:10–11)

## The Power of Grace

For those who believe in once saved always saved, this is a bitter drink to swallow. While giving lip service to the Scriptures, they refuse to accept them. Such believers turn the grace of God into a soft, passive, convenient kind of love, rather than the power of God that enables us to obey. Remember, God can keep you from falling. He can give you the power to change and the power to love Him. The question is, are you willing to fall to the ground and die?[9] Are you willing to hate your own life, hate your father and mother, give up everything, hate and despise money, deny yourself and pick up a cross?[10] Are you willing to do all these things? Do you really want God to work this saving obedience? For now, just read God's description of His grace.

> For the grace of God that brings salvation has appeared to all men. It teaches us to say "No" to ungodliness and worldly passions, and to live self-controlled, upright and godly lives in this present age, while we wait for the blessed hope—the glorious appearing of our great God and Savior, Jesus Christ, who gave himself for us to redeem us from all wickedness and to purify for himself a people that are his very own, eager to do what is good. (Titus 2:11–14)

God declared that His grace provides the power to "say 'No' to ungodliness." It is the power to deny self and the power to follow the directions of the Holy Spirit. When a man honestly surrenders to the grace of God, you will find rich obedience to the commands and ways of God in his life. If God's grace is absent, you will find rebellion and stubbornness toward His commands as you do in a once saved church. Scriptures are culturalized and apply only to things in the past.

You do not find a group of people "eager to do what is good" in those who believe once saved always saved. Instead, you find stubbornness toward any thought that someone might actually have to obey God with regard to one's salvation. Their doctrines are locked in place, their ways predictable, and you can spot them miles away. They want His "mercy," but never offer themselves to God's obedience as "living sacrifices." They do not have a true spiritual worship but have created a righteousness completely different from what God demands. This may sound like a broad and sweeping judgment but, if you are serious in investigating the proof for this, obtain a copy of the book *The Essential*

*Piece.*[11] However, be warned. It is not easy or comfortable reading.

> Therefore, I urge you, brothers, in view of God's mercy, to offer your bodies as living sacrifices, holy and pleasing to God—this is your spiritual act of worship. (Romans 12:1)

## At the Core

This core problem explains why so many people believe in once saved always saved. They want salvation, yet they also want to keep their lives. They want mercy, but without true surrender. For them, grace leads to an indulgence of sin, a covering over of sin, not the empowerment to overcome it. Therefore, those who believe in eternal security do not allow God to "purify" them. Simply stated, they remain too stiff-necked and resistant to the Holy Spirit. Every time they are challenged on some aspect of their lives, they say, "What are you talking about? I'm saved!" If they give this reaction to men, one can only shudder at the stubbornness they take into the prayer closet.

Eternal security forces anyone who believes in it to be so defensive and self-centered that they cannot take Scripture at face value. Often, when discussing this issue, I will just quote a verse without making any other comment. Of course, they immediately claim that it is "out of context," or that Jesus didn't really mean what He said. If there is one thing such people enjoy more than Scripture, it is their own opinion. They love to make up their own little scenarios to prove once saved always saved true. Next time you find yourself in a discussion with someone who believes in once saved always saved, agree that neither side will use any analogies or illustrations to make their arguments, and watch the frustration level rise. Chances are, they will not even be able to articulate their position. They would rather make up their own parables than surrender to the parables of Jesus.

Indeed, God's grace, if accepted on His terms, causes us to shake in holy fear. If we can lose our salvation, then naturally we should tremble. God's Word declares that we must have a holy fear. In the context of obeying, fear and trembling become a reality. Notice how the word "work" is used without any qualms by Paul. Yet to quote this passage to a eternal security person would produce a knee jerk reaction that yells, "See you are making this a matter of works. You used the very word, works, yourself." Never mind that we only quoted Scripture.

> Therefore, my dear friends, as you have always obeyed—not only in my presence, but now much more in my absence—continue to work out your salvation with fear and trembling, (Philippians 2:12)

Where you find belief in once saved always saved, you find smugness and self-righteousness. Where you find a people full of the true Grace of God you find "fear and trembling." Where you find a people who understand by the Holy Spirit the value of the grace of God, you find a people busy to "work out" their salvation. Now, must I stop and justify the word "work?" Did any of the writers of the New Testament stop and explain themselves every time they mentioned work or obedience?

However, as Jesus often sighed, so with a sigh I will state this once again. This is *not* a work that earns salvation, nor does it involve a fear of making one wrong step and losing your salvation. It is a balanced, reasonable, and joyful fear in Jesus. For no one loses their salvation because they stumble in one step. Once saved always saved waters down the fear of God to only lip service. In truth, such teaching omits honest, Holy Spirit inspired fear that also understands the "forgiveness" of God. God's power to forgive or not forgive causes us to fear Him in a holy way.

> If you, O Lord, kept a record of sins, O Lord, who could stand? But with you there is forgiveness; therefore you are feared. (Psalms 130:3–4)

## House Full of Grace

Think of God's grace as a house or household. A home is filled with many good things, like love and joy. Yet, the family has respect for the father and the rules of the house. Parents never kick a child out of a house because he stumbled in one small way against a rule. When my children made mistakes, or even sinned, I did not throw them out of the house. I brought them to repentance. If they had refused to repent, their soft hearts would have hardened and, over time, that would have cost them the privilege of living in our house. No more than I would permit one son bent on rebellion to destroy a home, will a God of justice allow the unfruitful to destroy His house. There comes a moment in time when, if a person remains bent on going to hell, God's mercy will simply stop. In short we must be found worthy. But those who believe in eternal security rightly declare no one is worthy. They are blinded to how someone can be unworthy of God's grace and still need to prove themselves worthy of entering heaven.

> But those who are considered worthy of taking part in that age and in the resurrection from the dead . . . (Luke 20:35)

Over time, as a person hardens his heart instead of repenting of those small missteps, he will fall away. As a side note, it only appears like a small mistake can cost someone his salvation because of our unspiritual minds. We cannot see what goes on behind the scenes and in the heart. As a result, many congregations find themselves caught by surprise when someone leaves their church and falls heavily into sin. They are unspiritual concerning their own sins and therefore cannot see the seriousness of sin in others. This is why Jesus said we must be faithful in little.[12] Therefore, Paul wrote the following passage to Timothy.

> Nevertheless, God's solid foundation stands firm, sealed with this inscription: "The Lord knows those who are his," and, "Everyone who confesses the name of the Lord must turn away from wickedness." In a large house there are articles not only of gold and silver, but also of wood and clay; some are for noble purposes and some for ignoble. If a man cleanses himself from the latter, he will be an instrument for noble purposes, made holy, useful to the Master and prepared to do any good work. (2 Timothy 2:19–21)

A house contains things used for "ignoble" purposes. If a man "cleanses himself" from these things he will become "noble" in the Lord, "holy, useful" and full of God's grace. Likewise, many in God's household believe in once saved always saved and are, therefore, used for ignoble purposes. Only those who cleanse themselves from doctrines that produce bad fruit will receive a rich welcome into the kingdom of heaven. For they understand the sheer joy of working out one's salvation with fear and trembling.

**The Deception**

Don't be deceived. Those who believe in eternal security cannot work out their salvation with fear and trembling. It is impossible to have such an attitude if you believe nothing you can do will cause you to lose that salvation. This is another major problem with once saved always saved. One lie inevitably leads to another. For, while such people claim to work out their salvation with fear and trembling, they remain full of pride and self-righteousness. Often they will try to "interpret" that Scripture as referring to some kind of heavenly reward, and not actual salvation. They would rather twist and mock God's Word than accept the truth. After all, when was the last time you heard anyone weeping with fear and trembling because they lost a heavenly reward or two? I am sure the reader has never seen an altar call for individuals to come forward who have lost some of the rewards that were theirs in heaven. Even if Scripture truly meant what they claim it does, they still don't live it! Believers in eternal security are complete hypocrites.

You will simply never meet a humble advocate of once saved always saved. They will always fail the test of humility. For, no matter what sin you bring to these people, it holds no eternal importance. They are saved and that's all there is to it. Conviction is cut off at the start and they never discover the blessings of true repentance. They have become haughty, self-righteous, and self-assured by misusing the very blood of Jesus they claim to have faith in.

# Chapter 6

# Thorn Bushes and Briers

No good tree bears bad fruit, nor does a bad tree bear good fruit. Each tree is recognized by its own fruit. People do not pick figs from thorn bushes, or grapes from briers. (Luke 6:43–44)

Bad doctrine produces a bad life and a bad life chooses bad doctrine. For this reason, Scripture calls us to watch our lives and doctrines closely. If we only check our doctrine, we will deceive ourselves about our lives. And watching only our lives is to ignore doctrine in favor of what we want to do. We have already looked at the doctrine of once saved always saved and some of the bad fruit it produces. Now we will take a closer look at the practical implications.

The fruit of this doctrine resembles a thorn bush or brier—a bush that intertwines itself among the good grapes of God and slowly chokes out the branches. The good fruit slowly dies and, as Jesus predicted, the love of most grows cold. It is no surprise that Jesus wondered if He would find faith on the earth when He returns. Eternal security was part of what Jesus saw coming that would stop true faith and cool the love of most in the church.

Like any thorn bush or brier, this doctrine has quickly swept over the world, choking out true discipleship in Jesus. Indeed, those few who do find a measure of true faith in Christ have to reach in very carefully to find only a small cluster of grapes or figs. By God's grace, He enables them to come to Him despite the thorns and briers. In short, God works in spite of those who preach once saved always saved, but not through them.

## Pride and Arrogance

The thorns of this doctrine affect the heart, actions, and soul of the church. The current sad condition of the church results from those who have made it sinfully easy to accept Jesus Christ as Lord and Savior. As Jesus stated, "wisdom is proved right by all her children" and the children of once saved always saved have proven to be a rebellious bunch. So what is the bad fruit of eternal security? Some of this we have already touched upon, but let's lay it all out clearly.

- It has made the church stiff-necked and arrogant.

  But they did not listen to me or pay attention. They were stiff-necked and did more evil than their forefathers. (Jeremiah 7:26)

Often, when confronted with the sins that this doctrine allows into the church, those who defend once saved always saved will point to saints of old considered as "pillars" of the church. But whether they are really pillars—or, indeed, really saints—or not, no man can truly say. Many that appear to us as great men of faith may prove the least of all. After all, Jesus said many who are first will be last and Paul told us to "judge nothing before the appointed time." The truth of the situation is this. Many of the men, such as Calvin, credited with establishing the doctrine of eternal security formulated their ideas in reaction to the other errors and heresies of their time. However, without the cross to crucify their own opinions, they simply rejected one extreme and grasped hold of another.

> It is good to grasp the one and not let go of the other. The man who fears God will avoid all extremes. (Ecclesiastes 7:18)

These saints were simply wrong about once saved always saved. While their own lives may or may not have reflected the bad fruit we see today, God will still hold them accountable for planting the seed. Remember that the bad fruit of a thorn or brier starts with a bad seed. Their small seed of bad doctrine results in a church today weighed down by arrogance.

Think about it. Which commands of God does the church actually obey today? Everything has become relative to each person and each church, with everyone choosing exactly what they want to believe and how they want to do things. You do not find the cross moving people in a direction they do not want to go, or bringing them to accept the truth in spite of what they want to believe. The truth is, those who believe in eternal security explain away far more Scripture than they actually obey.

The church has regressed to little more than elementary altar calls and pointing out the faults of others in a desperate attempt to get individuals saved. Once saved always saved stiffens the necks of those who hear the Word. They cannot turn their heads in any other direction in order to see anything else in Scripture. Indeed, they run out and keep away all who try to suggest we have more to obey in Jesus. They explain away any uncomfortable command as "cultural." The ways of God turn into mere suggestions and, if a man dares push for more, he is immediately labeled as preaching salvation by works. Like children who hum with their fingers in their ears, they refuse to hear Jesus calling for more.

Individuals or churches can do things any way they want, because nothing is a "salvation issue" anymore. Suggest otherwise and you will be branded a legalist. The lives of those who call for revival, yet believe in once saved always saved overflow with hypocrisy.

They call for revival in the music industry but listen to worldly music. They call for revival in doctrine but refuse to give up once saved always saved. They call for revival in the book publishing arena, but promote themselves in their own books. They call for revival in the church, but do not understand the results of real revival. They call for revival in others, but refuse to repent of things presented to them. What started out as a small evil now overruns the church, and the best church you can think of remains nothing more than a thorn bush or brier compared to what Jesus desires. So much "confusion" now fills our churches because we will not stand up for truth and obedience, except for what each church considers their pet doctrines and issues. We refuse to make anything a "salvation issue" and thus nothing is a salvation issue.

> The best of them is like a brier, the most upright worse than a thorn hedge. The day of your watchmen has come, the day God visits you. Now is the time of their confusion. (Micah 7:4)

Everyone finds the flavor of church they like. They settle in and shut out any challenge to their self-righteousness because, after all, it's not as if they could lose their salvation over it!

- Eternal security justifies the wide gate that leads to destruction.

Enter through the narrow gate. For wide is the gate and broad is the road that leads to destruction, and many enter through it. (Matthew 7:13)

The way most people become "Christians" today was totally unheard of in the New Testament.[1] The first church never thought, taught, or prompted anyone to "just ask Jesus into your heart." The idea of saying a canned prayer and signing the back page of a Bible would have caused an outpouring of condemnation. But the once saved always saved doctrine has found its niche. It sets up a concession stand right beside the wide gate that leads to destruction, offering fun, soft salvation, and easy altar calls.

When the crowds asked Peter what they had to do to be saved, he replied, "Repent and be baptized for the forgiveness of sins." But those who preach once saved always saved obviously don't think such an answer is good enough. In fact, they get indignant and angry at even the suggestion of "doing something" to be saved, since that implies that salvation depends on something that we do. Of course, they don't even see the obvious hypocrisy that even saying the "sinner's prayer" is doing something. Stubbornness so fills their hearts that they cannot even stand in unity with Peter.

During a radio interview about the insanity in the church,[2] the announcer realized that I preach the same salvation message as Peter. He went ballistic. Indeed, he would not shut up, but kept running over my words. Finally, in exasperation, I said, "Just say the words that Peter declared. Can you do it? Without adding any comments before or after, can you say with Peter, 'Repent and be baptized, every one of you, in the name of Jesus Christ for the forgiveness of your sins. And you will receive the gift of the Holy Spirit'?"[3]

He could not repeat Peter's words. It was impossible for him, as it is with most of the church today. All because eternal security robs the gospel of any of the demands that Jesus Himself set down. Bushels full of rotten fruit fill the Lord's orchard and their inability to be in unity with Peter and all of the Apostles shows the depth of rebellion. After all, it shouldn't be that hard to just say the words. But they cannot even mock them, for to do so would be to undermine and destroy their wide road understanding of salvation.

According to those who preach once saved always saved, all a person needs to do to be saved is sign a form, claim Jesus as their Savior, or bow their head and say a canned prayer—as long as they are "sincere," of course. The worm that bores its way into the apple creates such a rotten environment for the Spirit of Jesus that now some even maintain that one does not even have to ask Jesus into their heart. More and more churches teach that man literally does not have to "do" anything to be saved. After all, if a person is one of the elect, then their salvation is already assured. In reality, once saved always saved rejected God's "do" in favor of doing something easy and comfortable, and now that fruit has turned so rotten that the "do" disappears altogether.

No longer does a person have to sit down and count the cost of salvation.[4] Instead, they "come on down" to claim their prize as in a game show. As foretold in the Scriptures, a large host of insincere individuals now fill the church because of the fruit of eternal security.[5]

To demand and order people to obey the commands of God is thought of as bringing back the curse of the Law. No longer do we find pastors with authority from the Holy Spirit to crack a whip or command doctrines not to be preached.[6] A person preaching once saved always saved could never "order" followers to be water baptized—let alone someone who already had the Holy Spirit.

> So he ordered that they be baptized in the name of Jesus Christ. Then they asked Peter to stay with them for a few days. (Acts 10:48)

Gone is any authority in the Holy Spirit to powerfully speak and command the things of God. And we are only looking at one of the first and most basic of commands that Jesus gave. If stubbornness reigns supreme over this most elementary commandment, one can only shudder at the appalling sin of stubbornness eternal security has created.

Instead, we hang onto our opinions and have a zeal only for compromise. Indeed, the enthusiasm of most "Christians" for God seems no stronger than what they feel at a big sporting event. If you don't think this is true, read the book entitled *Insanity in the Church* and you will discover a whole host of Scriptures that the church does not obey, and has no desire to follow.

## Asleep in Their Pews

- Once saved always saved has put the soul and spirit to sleep in the church.

. . . for it is light that makes everything visible. This is why it is said: "Wake up, O sleeper, rise from the dead, and Christ will shine on you." (Ephesians 5:14)

Who wants to get out of bed when they feel all warm and comfortable? This is precisely what once saved always saved does. It gives the church a nice cozy, warm bed to lie in.

If this were not so serious, it would be laughable to hear someone who believes in once saved always saved call for revival and purity. After all, why should anyone repent? What does it matter if the person repents or not, if their salvation remains intact? How foolish it is to call for revival when the very act of obeying is considered falling under law. Their call for revival acts like an alarm clock that wakes everyone up, just so they can go back to sleep. Do you want to know what kind of revival preacher people really enjoy? The kind with a snooze button. People love to listen to a strong, emotional sermon, and then hit the snooze button so they can go right back to sleep. As a result, after all the recent years of prayers and efforts for revival, the church remains deader than ever. Everyone enjoys going back to sleep too much to wake up and honestly carry their cross for Jesus. The flesh loves nothing more than stealing a few more minutes of sleep. Therefore these preachers stay popular within their circles.

Such people may wake up for a few moments, but then they just sink back into a deeper sleep of self-assurance. After all, what is more comfortable than eternal security? Why *should* they wake up, let alone even think of getting out of bed? They convince themselves that they know the righteousness and holiness from God, after all, didn't they just hear a powerful sermon on righteousness? Such preachers tell themselves that they proclaim a tough gospel, but they do not realize that they leave a person's self alive. Preach a tough sermon and you will be loved by most, but strike at the heart of a person's "self" and you will be accused of going too far.

Woe unto those preachers who demand righteousness while embracing once saved always saved, for they furnish people with a pillow of self-righteousness on which to sleep. They are like the worms that actively bore into the apple and deposit their eggs which hatch into thousands of worms that infest entire orchards. Whole denominations, ministries, and works of God have been ruined and weakened because these worms actively preach eternal security. There is nothing worse for the church than a tough talking preacher who believes in eternal security.

Make no mistake about it. You may consider yourself a zealous Christian who believes in once saved always saved but the bad fruit of that doctrine will ruin you, and others, in time. You will produce the bad fruit of laziness, self-righteousness, and haughtiness.

## Slowly Drifting Away

A person can fall away by simply drifting little by little away from the Lord. Inch by inch and small degree by small degree, he moves away from the narrow road and the crucified life. Therefore God calls us to "pay more careful attention" to what we have heard. Once saved always saved is the raft that men build to assure themselves they stay afloat in the Lord, but they drift further and further away from shore.

> We must pay more careful attention, therefore, to what we have heard, so that we do not drift away. (Hebrews 2:1)

Now that we are generations into the once saved always saved doctrine, the demands of Jesus have been all but forgotten by the church. In other words, the vast majority of those who claim to be Christians have not even heard what they should pay "more careful attention" to. When told these things, they retort, "But I am saved. I asked Jesus into my heart and you are just trying to place me under legalism."

When I was a small boy, the Air Force stationed my father on the island of Guam. People used to go down to the beach, float out on the water in rubber rafts, and soak up the sun. As they fell asleep, the soft current moved them out into the deep sea. They would wake up miles away from the beach and see no land in site. In the same way, if we don't stay awake and pay attention, we can easily just "drift away" from saving grace. Therefore, it is very important to avoid churches and ministries that believe in eternal security. For we know that doctrine affects our lives and, in churches that believe you cannot lose your salvation, drifting becomes a way of life. In fact, drifting is exalted as a life of faith, because to strive to stay close to shore would be branded as "works." Who should row for shore if rowing is a sin? Who should be on guard against the drift of a current if to pick up an oar would be to earn one's salvation?

The writer of Hebrews said that we should "encourage one another daily, as long it is called Today." But encourage in what? Do you know what to encourage and what to warn against? Can you do it in the power of the Holy Spirit?

> See to it, brothers, that none of you has a sinful, unbelieving heart that turns away from the living God. But encourage one another daily, as long as it is called Today, so that none of you may be hardened by sin's deceitfulness. We have come to share in Christ if we hold firmly till the end the confidence we had at first. (Hebrews 3:12–14)

How can a devotee of once saved always saved "see to it" when they do not believe someone can "turn[s] away from the living God" in the first place? One can only shudder in sad amazement at how many of the Lord's children are destroyed and dragged off into misery and sin because no one even sees this as a danger. It is comparable to a doctor who works in a hospital but doesn't believe any of his patients can die.

Here, the writer of Hebrews directs his warning to "brothers." In other words, he warns true believers to watch themselves so that they don't become "unbelieving" and turn away from the "living God." But, again, eternal security dismisses it as merely concerning our rewards in heaven. No wonder that encouragement has all but died out in churches, replaced with socializing instead. For how can a man or woman be encouraged against turning away from that which they do not believe is possible? A church that holds to once saved always saved obviously reads this passage as, "See to it, false brothers who were never really saved, that your unbelieving heart doesn't leave the church." Needless to say, it makes absolutely no sense.

The deceitfulness of sin has invaded and flourished in the church today. According to this doctrine, no one stands in any danger of losing their salvation if they tolerate sin in their lives. Remove the threat and the urgency fades. It is like looking at skin cancer and saying, "Never mind, it's only on the surface." Woe unto such churches for, when that fear disappears, the deceitful nature of sin begins to infect everything. The proof of this lies all around us.

When it is no longer called Today, we will be in eternity, and *then* we will have no need to encourage one another daily not to drift away from the Lord. But, instead, those who cling to once saved always saved find it easier to simply say, "Oh, they were never really saved anyway." What an unloving comment to make, and what an uncaring doctrine to uphold. What kind of callous heart would damn another to justify their own doctrine? Indeed, it breeds such coldness towards others that, when someone leaves the church, it no longer matters because they were "never really saved in the first place." These churches that believe in once saved always saved have become clanging cymbals without love.[7] And what a clanging cymbal eternal security is, it grates the ears and rattles the bones of those who must endure its bad effects.

As Hebrews just told us, sin is deceitful. We often do not see the things that enslave us. Therefore, it takes a strong church that understands the seriousness of sin and the value of God's salvation to keep individuals from drifting away. Without the Light of Christ, members fight against sin in the dark. The Light reveals sin for what it is—not something that just leads to the loss of personal rewards, but to the loss of heaven itself. Again, the writer of Hebrews warned us, "We have come to share in Christ *if* we hold firmly till the end the confidence we had at first."

# The Solution

O Lord, do not your eyes look for truth? You struck them, but they felt no pain; you crushed them, but they refused correction. They made their faces harder than stone and refused to repent. (Jeremiah 5:3)

God looked for truth, but the Israelites refused to repent. He struck, but they felt no pain. God crushed His children, but they refused correction. Such is the bad fruit of eternal security. God strikes, but such believers always feel self-assured that they are saved and in no grave danger. God crushes, but it is not a salvation issue. He looks for the truth, but they have no need to repent.

The only solution is to feel pain from the Lord, to let the nails of the crucified life do their work. Jesus wants us to let go of all of self, including our doctrines and pride. We only have to let Him crush us, to fall to the ground and die, and He will work the new life. We must realize that salvation is a process and it does not end until we have passed the test in this life.

When a man believes in once saved always saved he becomes numb to the conviction of God. He acts like a man who goes to the dentist with a bad tooth, receives a shot of Novocaine to ease the pain, and then gets up before the dentist repairs the tooth. He thinks that, because the pain disappeared, the tooth is healed and his concerns lifted. Of course, as soon as the Novocaine wears off the pain will return, but the trouble with those who believe in once saved always saved is that they just keep going back for more Novocaine.

If you want the solution then you must soften your heart. You must admit you need to be taught again and humbly let God teach by way of the cross. It will feel painful, just as the cross is painful, but the end result is the resurrected life.

People who cling to once saved always saved can feel no real pain about their sin because they feel saved no matter what they do. They must shake off this addiction to comfort and numbness if they desire true blessings from the Lord. For one of the true blessings of Jesus is to bless us by turning us from our sin.

> When God raised up his servant, he sent him first to you to bless you by turning each of you from your wicked ways. (Acts 3:26)

## The Fear of the Lord

The person who believes in eternal security has removed the fear that filled the first church. When we first come to the Lord there is, or ought to be, a realization of God's holiness and that he powerfully deals with sin. This fear, along with the kindness of God, motivates men to preach and to repent. As you can see below, Paul wrote that he knew what it means to "fear the Lord" so he preached to men.

> Since, then, we know what it is to fear the Lord, we try to persuade men. (2 Corinthians 5:11a)

Regardless of what the once saved always saved preachers claim, this fear is not in their lives. This is demonstrated by how fast and easily they pronounce someone a Christian. Often they subtly, or not so subtly, use the threat of hell to motivate people to say a believer's prayer. Of course, who wouldn't prefer to say a simple prayer rather than burn in hell?

This initial fear moves a man to repentance and the church to maturity. The bad fruit of shallow repentance, always occurs when we remove or downplay holy fear. This is what the once saved always saved doctrine has done to the church. No longer do we find groups of people stirred up to repent by the fear and kindness of God. Instead, the church entertains and bribes people into accepting Jesus Christ as Lord and Savior. Then, once they join a church, the fear of God does not grow and mature, indeed they avoid it at all cost and are assured by eternal security teachers that everything is just dandy.

> Then the church throughout Judea, Galilee and Samaria enjoyed a time of peace. It was strengthened; and encouraged by the Holy Spirit, it grew in numbers, living in the fear of the Lord. (Acts 9:31)

Such churches are not like the first church, "living in the fear of the Lord," but more like the whitewash church that cries out to God from their soft pews or couches. Oh, many of them will pride themselves on being tough against sin and contending for the truth, but they live a lie. They "strum away on harps like David and improvise on musical instruments," thinking they are a strong, worshipping people. They think they have the best of God, the choice lambs and fatted calves, but they remain haughty and self-content. They cannot grieve over their ruin, because they do not see the serious consequences of their sin. After all, if a man has faith in Jesus and can never lose his salvation, how bad could the consequences be? This attitude frees them to have a good time, drink wine by the bowlful, soothe over every Scripture, and smooth out every rough aspect of the cross with the finest of lotions.

> You lie on beds inlaid with ivory and lounge on your couches. You dine on choice lambs and fattened calves. You strum away on your harps like David and improvise on musical instruments. You drink wine by the bowlful and use the finest lotions, but you do not grieve over the ruin of Joseph. Therefore you will be among the first to go into exile; your feasting and lounging will end. (Amos 6:4–7)

Certainly, a lot of crying out for revival and discussion about righteousness rises, but all from a comfortable padded pew. They "wail upon their beds" as Hosea wrote. They cry alright, but from a position of false hope and comfort as they gather together for "new wine" and for "grain" in the name of Jesus. They falsely believe they have the Holy Spirit (new wine) and the Bible (grain) but they lie asleep in the name of the Lord and continue to turn away from the commands of the Lord.

> They do not cry out to me from their hearts but wail upon their beds. They gather together for grain and new wine but turn away from me. (Hosea 7:14)

The only solution is to let the painful, crucifying cross come and do its work—a cross that will move them out of their comfortable pews to suffer in their bodies and be done with sin. The cross will deal a deathblow to the easy, 1-2-3, "just ask Jesus into your heart," wide gate gospel calls. Instead, it will place people on the narrow road.

Once a young man joined our church who grew up believing in eternal security. Rather, than challenging him straight away on the issue, we completely ignored it and simply taught him the offensive message of the cross. He continued to grow in his relationship with God, picking up the cross God had for him and one day came bounding out of his prayer time exclaiming, "I can't believe I ever believed in once saved always saved!" He felt appalled not only at himself but at his teachers who had led him astray. This is the nature of the true cross. A person is truly taught by God.[1]

## Like Christ

When the church finally lets God be God they can once again say with Peter that all Christians everywhere need the same "attitude" as that of Jesus Christ. An attitude which knows the only way to salvation lies with suffering against sin by the grace of God. After all, only those who overcome stand with Jesus in heaven. Only those who suffer with Christ are "done with sin." Talk about a concept that overwhelms the believer of eternal security with objections of salvation by works—this is it. No wonder that sin is rampant in a church where eternal security is embraced.

Therefore, since Christ suffered in his body, arm your-selves also with the same attitude, because he who has suffered in his body is done with sin. As a result, he does not live the rest of his earthly life for evil human desires, but rather for the will of God. (1 Peter 4:1–2)

As a result of this honest understanding of the crucified life, Peter tells us we overcome sin and live for "the will of God." Among those who believe in once saved always saved a lazy, self-satisfied attitude replaces one of suffering. It could be no other way, for belief in eternal security produces complacency in a man even as he denies his complacent attitude. Sloppy faith replaces effort and false rest replaces hard work. The once saved always saved teacher becomes slothful without realizing it.

This leads them to become more concerned about their lives, their ministry and their wants. They use the members of the church, as Jesus puts it, they beat the servants of God for their own spiritual goals. Though they call Jesus Lord and have the hope of being put in charge "of all his possessions," they are later assigned a place with "unbelievers." Again, Jesus is clear that a man can fall away. The man in this parable was once in the household of God but, in the end, is placed with unbelievers.

The Lord answered, "Who then is the faithful and wise manager, whom the master puts in charge of his servants to give them their food allowance at the proper time? It will be good for that servant whom the master finds doing so when he returns. I tell you the truth, he will put him in charge of all his possessions. But suppose the servant says to himself, 'My master is taking a long time in coming,' and he then begins to beat the menservants and maidservants and to eat and drink and get drunk. The master of that servant will come on a day when he does not expect him and at an hour he is not aware of. He will cut him to pieces and assign him a place with the unbelievers. (Luke 12:42–46)

Every excuse and justification will be "cut" to "pieces" and that believer put with pagans in hell. All because he began to become lazy, feeding his belly and taking advantage of others for his own goals and purposes.

## Torment a Blessing

When God convicts, crushes, and comes against our sin time and time again, we gain a powerful blessing. One of my greatest joys is to be convicted about my sin and to let the Holy Spirit not only forgive but empower me to overcome that sin. That conviction might last a day, a week, or even years, but it is the blessing of God poured out into my life. Indeed, Paul felt blessed when God sent a demon to keep him from sin.

> To keep me from becoming conceited because of these surpassingly great revelations, there was given me a thorn in my flesh, a messenger of Satan, to torment me. Three times I pleaded with the Lord to take it away from me. But he said to me, "My grace is sufficient for you, for my power is made perfect in weakness." Therefore I will boast all the more gladly about my weaknesses, so that Christ's power may rest on me. (2 Corinthians 12:7–9)

God sent the demon to prevent sin, not as punishment for any actual sin Paul had committed. Why did God go to these lengths to keep Paul from pride? So that he would not lose his salvation. Remember how Paul wrote in 1 Timothy 3:6 that a church leader "must not be a recent convert, or he may become conceited and fall under the same judgment as the devil." Satan's sin was pride and his judgment will be hell. Satan fell from the grace of heaven and God did not want Paul to become prideful and fall under the same judgment. A follower of once saved always saved, however, admits no possibility of falling under the same judgment as Satan, and therefore he has no real need to guard against pride. As a result, he actually celebrates pride as a virtue.

Paul understood that he, and every church leader, could come under the same judgment as Satan, losing heaven and gaining hell.

Paul was no fool concerning the issue of salvation. He "gladly" accepted this blessing from God, even when it came in the form of a tormenting demon. How much more should all true Christians look for God's cleansing blessings to flow? But eternal security cuts off that power of the cross to crucify unto the resurrected life. It makes hell an empty threat and puts up a barrier between the blessings of God and the man He wants to purify and place on solid ground.

**Lawless Men**

Peter warns that we must be "on guard" against these "lawless" men. These lawless men are like the worms who find a weak spot in the flesh of an apple to bore in and plant their eggs. They may be nice, you may call them brother; they may be great teachers; they may discern the faults of others, but they deposit the eggs of a doctrine that will eat away at the good fruit God is trying to grow.

> Bear in mind that our Lord's patience means salvation, just as our dear brother Paul also wrote you with the wisdom that God gave him. He writes the same way in all his letters, speaking in them of these matters. His

letters contain some things that are hard to understand, which ignorant and unstable people distort, as they do the other Scriptures, to their own destruction. Therefore, dear friends, since you already know this, be on your guard so that you may not be carried away by the error of lawless men and fall from your secure position. But grow in the grace and knowledge of our Lord and Savior Jesus Christ. To him be glory both now and forever! Amen. (2 Peter 3:15–18)

What unusual wording Peter uses. How does one "fall" from a "secure position?" If it is secure, how is there a possibility that one could fall? The answer is simple; by listening to the "error of lawless men." Again we see God, through Peter, using the word "fall." Falling from one's security in Christ. If you stand on the solid rock of Jesus be careful of lawless men who cause you to lose your balance. Watch out for those who rob you of the grace that enables you to stand upon the rock, Jesus Christ.

No wonder the catch-all excuse for those who teach once saved always saved is that they do not want to "fall under legalism." Lawless men always fight hard against obedience, for they are in their heart lawless against the crucified life. At heart, they are not really concerned about legalism, but try to hide the fact that they are lawless men. After all, we can easily deal with legalism. One doesn't have to whine, scream, shout, or object to every Scripture that demands obedience to keep from falling under legalism.

Again, this is not a case of merely stumbling. A man must choose to leave his secure position. Those that hide under the shelter of the Lord will certainly remain safe. Lawless men can pull you from it *only* if you give way to them. Run to the name of the Lord, believing in your heart and confessing with your mouth everyday with true surrender and you will find safety.

> The name of the Lord is a strong tower; the righteous run to it and are safe. (Proverbs 18:10)

The solution to this problem is to call them to repentance, and if they will not repent to leave them. Indeed, they will kick you out anyway if you stand firm in the truth that one can lose their salvation. If there is one thing a once saver cannot endure, it is someone who believes that salvation can be lost. The solution is to reject lawless men, reject the itching ear doctrine of once saved, pick up a cross and honestly begin to follow Jesus. To allow Jesus to plow up unplowed ground and to level ground that is overgrown with the weed of eternal security.[2]

*Chapter 8*

# The Fearful Estate of Francis Spira

The sins of some men are obvious, reaching the place of judgment ahead of them; the sins of others trail behind them. (1 Timothy 5:24)

Some men's sins reach "the place of judgment ahead of them." In other words, they feel the fires of judgment before they die. The following true account has been passed around since 1638. It is a story of a man who gave up his salvation for comfort, money, and acceptance by the church. With some reluctance I include this story, for Scripture alone should be sufficient to convince us of the error of once saved always saved. But if God has provided this example, we do well to heed it. We shortened, edited and updated the language of this man's sad judgment—which reached him ahead of time.

- **The Fearful Estate of Francis Spira
  By Nathaniel Bacon April 6, 1638**

In 1548, during the reign of Edward VI of England, in the town of Citadella, Italy, lived Francis Spira, a Civil Lawyer. He was well known for being a very learned and composed sort of a man. He had a wife and eleven children and they lived wealthy, abundant lives. He said of himself, "I was excessively covetous of money and I lived accordingly to get on in the world by injustice. I corrupted justice with deceit and invented tricks to deceive justice. I would either dishonestly defend good causes or I would deceitfully sell them to my opponent. I maintained bad causes with all of my strength, willingly opposing the known truth. I either betrayed or perverted any trust given to me."

When Luther revised his opinions on the Scriptures, Spira couldn't resist examining them himself (being the man of learning that he was). He began to search the Scriptures and any books of controversy he could find, old and new alike. Spira began to take these teachings on as his own with such a zeal that he became a teacher of them, first to his wife and children, then to his friends and acquaintances. He seemed to neglect everything other than to impress his point to others that we must wholly and only depend on the free and unchangeable love of God in the death of Christ, as the only way to salvation. He continued in this teaching and took a stand against the Roman Catholic Church for about six years.

At this point the Roman Catholic clergy realized that the selling of their pardons was decreasing and their purgatory becoming less popular. At first they glossed over the issue with accusations against Luther and then they more specifically began to point the finger at Spira. In order to get other clergymen on their side against him they prom-

ised work for some, do favors for others, and offer kindness to others. Their aim was to separate Spira's soul from
his body, or both from God, by any means possible.

Determined to put a stop to Spira, they summoned the
help of a man named John Casa, the Pope's legate resident
at Venice, a man thoroughly against the Protestants. The
clergymen told him that Spira condemned the church. He
was learned in the Scriptures and an eloquent speaker. Spira
was a dangerous Lutheran who could not be ignored.

Faced with the full force of persecution, Spira was now
left with only three options: He could either apostatize and
give up his life as a lie; he could endure the malice of his
enemies; or he could leave his wife, children, friends and
possessions and flee to a foreign country in voluntary exile
where he would suffer misery after misery. These things
weighed on his mind but eventually he grew afraid of losing his family and his wealth, and so the cares of this world
and the deceitfulness of riches choked the seed that grew
in his heart.

Spira then went to John Casa to apologize, admitted his
error and folly in what he had taught to others, and asked
for forgiveness. At this point Casa demanded that a paper
of all Spira's errors be written and then commanded Spira
to sign it. Casa then commanded Spira to return to his own
town to declare this confession, acknowledging the whole
doctrine of Rome to be holy and true, and to declare the
teachings of Luther and other such heretics as false and
damnable.

While Spira prepared for this journey home, he found
himself thinking not about what great testimony he had
given of his faith, but how he had denied Christ and His
gospel in Venice and now on his way to do so in his own
country. He heard a voice say to him, "Spira, what are you

doing here? Where are you going? Do you think eternal life so insignificant that you prefer this life? Is it good to prefer your wife and children to Christ? Is the applause of men better than the glory of God? Are the possessions of this world more dear to you than the salvation of your own soul? Is the blasphemous lie of one moment more desirable than dreadful eternal wrath? Think about what Christ endured for your sake. Shouldn't you suffer something for Him? Remember, man, that the sufferings of this life are nothing compared to the glory that will be revealed. If you suffer for His sake, you will also reign with Him. You cannot answer for what you have already done but, nevertheless, the gate of mercy is not quite shut. Take heed that you don't heap sin upon sin, otherwise you will repent when it is too late."[1]

Even though he knew clearly that he forsook the gospel, Spira continued the process which would restore him to the church and his family. He recited his paper in front of an assembly of around two thousand people and was fined thirty pieces of gold. He was then sent home to his goods, his wife, and his children.

Soon afterwards, Spira heard the voice again telling him that he had denied the Lord for "thirty pieces of silver" and had denied the truth of God. The voice condemned him to the sentence of eternal damnation. At this, Spira fell down, his body and his mind trembling and quaking. Although his body soon calmed, he never did find any peace of mind and continued on in excessive torments, professing that the revenging hand of God held him captive. He knew then that he was completely undone and that he could neither hope for grace nor Christ's intercession with God on his behalf.

His friends believed him subject to some kind of madness. They took him to Padua and enlisted the help of both great physicians and pious diviners who came to the conclusion that Spira's symptoms were caused by some grief. None of their skills could change anything and so Spira said to them, "Do you think that this disease is to be cured by potions? Believe me, there is no medicine! Because neither potions nor drugs can help a weak soul that is cast down with a sense of sin and the wrath of God. Only Christ must be the true Physician, and the Gospel the only Antidote." They readily believed him once he explained the truth of the whole situation, and they urged him to seek some kind of spiritual comfort.

By this time, Spira's fame had spread all over Padua and the neighboring country, partly because of the disease, but primarily because he had shown such remorse for standing before the church and rejecting Lutheran doctrine. Many people came to see him, some out of curiosity to talk to him and others out of a pious desire to try to comfort him again.

His own friends criticized him and asked him what he believed caused his disease. Contrarily, they tried to comfort him with God's promises in the Scriptures and examples of His mercy but Spira replied, "My sin is now unworthy of God's mercy."

"No" they answered, "the mercy of God is above all sin. God wants all men to be saved."

"That is not true" said Spira, "He would have all men that He has elected to be saved. He would not allow a damned reprobate to be spared and I'm telling you that I am one of their number. I know it, for I willingly, against my knowledge and belief, denied Christ before men, both in private and in public. My hardened heart will not allow me to hope."

In the silence that followed, someone asked him if he really did believe the doctrine that he was accused of teaching. Again there was a long silence before he answered, "I did believe it when I denied it, but now I neither believe that nor the doctrine of the Roman Church. I believe nothing. I have no faith, no trust, and no hope. I am a reprobate like Cain or Judas, who trampled all hope of mercy and fell into despair. My heart is dead and cold, and it was so from the beginning, though I believed that Luther was right and Rome was wrong."

They began to rebuke him claiming that he had not violated the mercy of God. He refused all comfort and said that God's mercy only extends to the elect and not to people like him, who are deservingly sealed up for wrath. Then they reminded him that Christ came to take away sin. To this Spira answered, "This is indeed comforting to the elect, but as for a wretch like me it brings nothing but grief and torment because I condemned it. That makes me as guilty of nailing Jesus to the cross as Judas Iscariot."

Spira then became overcome with grief. He tossed himself up and down upon the bed. The violence of these fits amazed many of the onlookers. Some of them whispered that he was possessed by demons.

"Do you doubt it?" He said overhearing them. "I have a whole legion of devils that live within me and have taken me as their own, and justly too for I have denied Christ before men."

"Did you do that willingly, though?" they asked.

"That is not the point," said Spira, "Christ said whoever denies me before men, I will deny before my Father who is in heaven. Christ will not be denied and therefore even though I did not want to deny Him in my heart, the fact is I did."

Some asked him whether he thought there were worse pains than what he experienced now. He said that he knew there were far worse pains than those that he suffered. "For the wicked will rise to their judgment, but they will not stand in judgment; this makes me tremble when I think of it; yet I desire nothing more than that I might get to that place, where I will surely feel the worst, and so be freed from the fear of worse to come."

"No, good Francis," his friends said, "the devil is upon you. Don't let the seriousness of your sin (if it is serious) amaze you."

"You are right," replied Spira, "the devil has possessed me, and God has left me to his power, for I find I can neither believe the Gospel, nor trust in God's mercy. I have sinned against the Holy Ghost, and God has rightly handed me over to perpetual punishment, without any hope of pardon. It is true that the greatness of sin, or the multitude of sin, cannot bind God's mercy. All the many sins of my former life didn't trouble me so much because I trusted that God would not punish me for them. But I never repented for them by God's grace as I repented before the church. Now, since I have sinned against the Holy Ghost, God has taken all power of a true repentance away from me, and this brings all of my sins back to memory, and I say guilty of one, guilty of all. Therefore, it does not matter whether my sins are great or small, few or many, they are all sins where neither Christ's blood nor God's mercy belongs to me. God will have mercy on whom He will have mercy and will harden whom He will harden. That is what eats at my heart. He has hardened me and therefore I cannot do anything but despair."

"Your problem," said Gribauldus, "is not as uncommon as you make it. Job was so far gone that he complained that God had set a mark against him; and David, who was a man after God's own heart, often complained that God had forsaken him and had become his enemy; yet both received comfort again. Therefore, comfort yourself and God will come in the end, even if He seems far away now."

"Oh brother," Spira answered, "I agree with you in all of this. The devils believe and tremble, but David was elected and loved by God; and even though he fell, God didn't completely take His Holy Spirit from him and so he was heard when he prayed, 'Lord, please don't take Your Holy Spirit from me.' But I, on the other hand, am forever banished from the presence of God.

Therefore, I know that I will live in hardness of heart as long as I live. Oh! That I might feel even the least sense of the love of God for me, even just for a moment, for now I feel His heavy wrath burning against me as if the torments of hell were within me. My desperation is hell itself."

With this Gribauldus said, "I really do believe, Spira, that now God has disciplined you in this life and corrected you in mercy here, that He might spare you after this, having mercies stored up for you in the time to come."

"No," replied Spira. "I already know that I am a reprobate because He has afflicted me with hardness of heart. Oh, how I wish that my body had suffered throughout my whole life so that He would be pleased to release my soul and ease my burdened conscience."

With many other arguments they tried to convince Spira until eventually he cried out, "It is wonderful how I desire to pray to God with all my heart, and all my strength, and yet I can't. I see my damnation and know that the only remedy is in Christ and yet I can't make myself lay hold of it because this is one of the punishments of the damned. They confess the same as I do, they repent of their loss of heaven and they envy the elect, yet that selfish repentance does them no good, for they can't change any of it without grace."

At this time two bishops came in with some scholars of the University. They wanted to pray the Lord's Prayer with Spira and he consented. "Our Father which art in Heaven," then breaking into tears Spira wailed, "I have been forsaken by God and can't call to him from my heart as I used to!"

But they went on. "Thy Kingdom come."

"Oh Lord," said Spira, "bring me also into this Kingdom; Please don't shut me out."

Then at the words "Give us this day our daily bread" he added, "Oh Lord, I have enough and abundance to feed this carcass of mine, but there is another bread. Above all things I humbly beg for the bread of Your grace, without which I know I am nothing but a dead man."

"Lead us not into temptation"

"Lord, the enemy has overcome me, seeing that I might escape. Please help me to overcome this cruel beast." Even after these prayers, though, Spira did not believe that God could give him His grace.

People from all over continued to visit Spira. Seldom less than twenty people sat with him at any one time. Spira exhorted them all: "Take heed, it is no light or easy matter to be a Christian. It is not Baptism or reading the Holy Scriptures, or boasting of your faith in Christ, even though these are good, that prove that you are a Christian. There must be conformity in your life to the Holy Word. A Christian must be strong, not carrying an obscure profession, expressing the image of Christ, and holding out against all opposition even until the last breath. He must be diligent in righteousness and holiness to make his calling and election sure."

One of his friends asked how it could be that Spira spoke so well on the judgments and grace of God and the Holy Spirit, and eagerly desires them, and yet at the same time believe that he was utterly deprived of them. But no matter how many discussions they had, Spira continued on in his sorrow. Often he would turn aside to certain people present and plead with them to watch their lives closely. "Remember the Word" he said, "that he who loves father, mother, brothers, sisters, sons, daughters, friends, houses or land more than Christ is not worthy of Him."

"These words," they said, "do not sound like the words of a wicked reprobate."

"Remember the rich glutton in the Gospel, who though in hell, was careful that his brethren should not come to the same place of torment as he had. Take heed Brethren of the miserable estate I am in."

Spira's friends watched him grow worse as he talked with the people around him. They decided together to carry him back to his own country. When one man suggested that they pray together before they leave, Spira refused, saying that he was separated from God since he grew more and more hard-hearted and that their prayers would not help him. And so they began their journey, Spira often said that he envied the condition of Cain or Judas.

He refused to eat except by force and even then he would not allow the food to digest. Vehemently desiring water to drink, ever pining, yet fearful to live long, in dread of hell, yet coveting death. In continual torment, yet his own tormentor, and thus consuming himself with grief and horror, impatience and despair, like a living man in hell, Spira represented an extraordinary example of the justice and power of God. His appearance reduced to nothing but a pile of sinews and bones.

One day with a ghastly look, Spira saw a knife lying on the table and ran to harm himself, but his friends stopped him. Whereupon with indignation he said, "I would I were above God, for I know he will have no mercy on me." Within a few days of his arrival home, he departed from this present life.

Take heed of backsliding, and keep a good conscience. A bad conscience is more to be feared than the Spanish Inquisition.

Spira lost his crown of life because he feared what he would have to suffer. However, few should chide him for this, because many more have lost the crown of life over less. Perhaps they disagreed with a doctrine, refused the voice of the Holy Spirit or objected to the cross they were given to carry. Remember well how many turned their backs on Jesus simply because His words offended them, not because the pressures of man were let loose on them.

> Do not be afraid of what you are about to suffer. I tell you, the devil will put some of you in prison to test you, and you will suffer persecution for ten days. Be faithful, even to the point of death, and I will give you the crown of life. (Revelation 2:10)

We must pause and ask the question again. How can a person or a church be on guard against losing something they believe they cannot lose? It would be like warning a homeowner to lock his doors when he thinks there is no danger of anyone breaking in. Indeed, in foolish pride, he would declare, "Oh, we don't need to lock our doors in this neighborhood." Jesus commands all of his disciples not to be so stupid. We have to fight to "hold on" to our "crown."

> I am coming soon. Hold on to what you have, so that no one will take your crown. (Revelation 3:11)

This is not a crown of rewards, but the crown of life. For this reason James wrote "Blessed is the man who perseveres under trial, because when he has stood the test, he will receive the *crown of life* that God has promised to those who love him."[2] Bottom line: unfaithful = no crown of life. But one has to compete for this crown according to God's rules. Man's religious ways and works cannot and will not save.[3] Take heed from this man's sad story that you too do not lose the crown of life.

Chapter 9

# If You Think You Are Falling Away

It is impossible for those who have once been enlightened, who have tasted the heavenly gift, who have shared
in the Holy Spirit, (Hebrews 6:4)

If you have fallen away from the Lord there is no point
in reading this chapter. It is impossible for you to repent and to be saved. For when a person has been enlightened, tasting the heavenly gift of grace and sharing in
fellowship with the Holy Spirit—if they fall away—to be
brought back again.  In fact, let us read on in Hebrews
through verses 5 and 6.

who have tasted the goodness of the word of God and
the powers of the coming age, if they fall away, to be
brought back to repentance, because to their loss they
are crucifying the Son of God all over again and subject-
ing him to public disgrace. (Hebrews 6:5–6)

If a man or woman tasted the power of God's Word and
the power "of the coming age" verse 6 tells us that they

cannot be "brought back to repentance." The reason God will not permit this is because Jesus would have to die a second time. To their "loss" they would force God to crucify "the Son of God all over again" and subject "him to public disgrace. But since God's Son is so precious to Him God would never permit such a unholy thing to take place. God would never have Jesus come to earth again and die on the cross just to allow someone to come back in who has fallen away. In other words, if a person doesn't value Jesus enough the first time they certainly would not the second time. Cheap grace always produces cheap attitudes towards what Jesus did on the cross. And in no greater arena does one find this unholy attitude than in the eternal security camp. This is why it is so important to understand that Jesus is a source of eternal salvation only for those who obey Him!

> and, once made perfect, he became the source of eternal salvation for all who obey him (Hebrews 5:9)

However, if you have been cut off from Jesus and have not yet reached that point, there remains a slim chance of hope. But you will need to make every effort, and I do mean *every effort,* to return.

You may have been cut off from the vine for any number of reasons. Or you may have wandered from the faith or chosen in some way not to remain in Jesus. However, you may still have enough "sap" to allow a grafting back in. When a branch withers it normally[1] does so slowly. This means there remains possible a brief period for repentance and return to the Lord. If you fail to seize that opportunity, you will be picked up and thrown into the fire and burned.

> If anyone does not remain in me, he is like a branch that is thrown away and withers; such branches are picked up, thrown into the fire and burned. (John 15:6)

We see this situation clearly in the letter Paul wrote to the Galatians. Paul flat out declared that they had "fallen away from grace."

> You who are trying to be justified by law have been alienated from Christ; you have fallen away from grace. (Galatians 5:4)

The spirit of Jesus will never put out a smoldering wick,[2] and so we see a rare offer of mercy. The Galatians killed the new birth of Jesus given to them. They had stopped the flow of mercy and grace that worked the new life and were cut off.

Paul sees their condition and responds with great zeal and urgency, something those who believe in eternal security cannot do. They cannot love like this because in their minds no such danger even exists. They are like people who stand by and don't even attempt to save a drowning man, because all they see is the surface and so they don't believe the water is deep enough to drown in.

Eternal security really is an excuse to live a selfish and loveless life. Those who believe in eternal security just do not have enough love to go through the pains of childbirth again with a fallen Christian. Because, in order for a person to come back to the Lord, someone must go through the "pains of childbirth" until Jesus again is "formed" in them. Note well the word "again." They had at one time gone through the pains that accompany being born again but along the way mortally wounded the new life.[3] For a person in such a condition to be restored, much pain, labor, prayer, and suffering will take place in those trying to restore the person to the new life of Christ.

> My dear children, for whom I am again in the pains of childbirth until Christ is formed in you, (Galatians 4:19)

Just as no baby can deliver itself and grow up to become a healthy child without help, so you cannot help yourself if you have fallen away. You must humble yourself and seek out those who can go through the requirements to have Christ formed in you again. This is no easy process and requires around the clock attention, fellowship, and prayer, until the heart softens again and pride breaks.

Most likely your doctrine will be corrected, the secret things of your heart laid bare, and action required to gain Jesus once again.

It is a matter of taking Jesus at His word when He declares that we should make "every effort"[4] to be saved. Below are a list of the efforts and steps required.

- Act today. Do not delay at the first tugging of grace. To refuse is to slip even further towards damnation.

- Admit the truth. Admit that you have fallen away. Lay your excuses and self-justification at the cross to be crucified. You stand in grave danger, and now is the time to give up all pretense of having something left in Jesus. There may be some sap left in you, but it dries up hour by hour. Don't be so foolish as to look at yourself and say, "Oh, here is some green, something good. Something of God in me." If you are cut off, you must fully see and admit that. Only then do you have any hope of being grafted back in again.

- Find someone skilled in "childbirth." Someone that can encourage and rebuke and guide you by the Holy Spirit through the periods of pain and rest that accompany labor.

- Prepare to leave everything. Act decisively and to do whatever it takes to have Christ again. Your heart and life will be dealt with and the cross will seek to put it to death. Be prepared to feel shocked, and to weep more than you ever have before. For to experience the resurrected life you must first be crucified.

- Confront your sin head on. Remember you are in this position because you failed to surrender something, or someone, before the Lord. God will bring into the Light, in front of others, such idols and sins. Prepare yourself to really learn what it means to walk in the Light.[5]

- Ignore your feelings, fears, and questions. The spiritual battle will grow intense. Satan will not let go easily. Desperately seek the help of others.

- Above all, do not accept a sloppy and easy faith or a "quick fix" solution. You must return to being saved by grace and not by the efforts of religious man. Do not associate with those who believe in eternal security for they will only pull you from the narrow road once again.

- All of this will take time. No baby grows up in one day. We do not consider a baby fully developed on the day of birth. It takes years of worry, watching, and caring before one can say a child is on safe ground. You must find a church that will point out when you start to drift away.

If you do not allow God to deal with the thorns and thistles that cut you off from Jesus, in the end you will be "burned." You are in grave danger of being cursed, so run and repent fully to Jesus. Then it will be said of you that "we are confident of better things in your case—things that accompany salvation."

> But land that produces thorns and thistles is worthless and is in danger of being cursed. In the end it will be burned. Even though we speak like this, dear friends, we are confident of better things in your case—things that accompany salvation. (Hebrews 6:8–9)

Do these things and you can say "Amen" to the final Scripture in this chapter. Fail to do so and your "Amen" will be judged for taking the Lord's name in vain, and added to the list of things that will torture you in hell.

Not only have we seen the obvious fact that men can fall from grace and become alienated from Christ, but we have also seen that, for a brief moment, when the Holy Spirit makes this reality clear, some backsliders can possibly repent. If you should find yourself in this position and you hear God telling you these words, do not harden your heart. Repent, with all energy and strength which God desires to work.[6] You have not a moment to lose. Begin now to tell the Lord you will surrender moment by moment to the leading of His voice and do all He commands and directs. Don't brush off the conviction or ignore the calling. This could be your last chance, for as Scripture says:

> As has just been said: "Today, if you hear his voice, do not harden your hearts as you did in the rebellion." (Hebrews 3:15)

Let us end by praising God, to whom all glory and power belongs. For, in Jesus, all glory, majesty, power, and authority reigns, and He, in the greatest of love and mercy, can keep you from falling from grace. He will graft you in and mature you, so that you will put complete confidence in Him who is able to keep you as you work out your salvation with fear and trembling.

To him who is able to keep you from falling and to present you before his glorious presence without fault and with great joy—to the only God our Savior be glory, majesty, power and authority, through Jesus Christ our Lord, before all ages, now and forevermore! Amen. (Jude 1:24–25)

Amen!

# Everything Said

Now that you know these things, stand firm against once saved always saved and grow in grace and knowledge.

Therefore, dear friends, since you already know this, be on your guard so that you may not be carried away by the error of lawless men and fall from your secure position. But grow in the grace and knowledge of our Lord and Savior Jesus Christ. To him be glory both now and forever! Amen. (2 Peter 3:17)

# Who Is Timothy Williams?

Because of the volatile nature of this topic, it is probably best to give some details about the author of this book. For some of those who do not want to believe the plain truth of Scripture that is here will inevitably attempt to avoid the issue by seeking to discredit the author.

Like the disciples, Timothy Williams is unschooled and ordinary.[1] He never attended Bible college. In fact, God called him to drop out of secular college and then began to press the cross into his life. The things you read here result from God working the foolishness of the cross. He grew up attending the Methodist church from time to time. He pastors a non-denominational church in Washington state and fellowships with all who love and embrace the offensive message of the cross. Below is a list of basic beliefs.

**Basic Beliefs**

We do not preach "ink," therefore the beliefs listed below are something alive and active by the power of the Holy Spirit, (2 Corinthians 3:3). Sound Doctrine is a church where everyone picks up the cross Jesus has for them. You are sure to find something you disagree with. We encourage you to first seek your own cross that God might deal with any flesh that would drive you away.

We agree with Jesus that:

- Love from the Holy Spirit is the most important matter. Love for God, our fellow man and family is the fruit of Jesus. A love that flows from a crucified life is full of truth and no compromise. (1 Corinthians 13:1–13; Luke 1:17; Matthew 10:34). Request the free sermon entitled "The Most Important Sermon" at www.freesd.org

- We are saved by true faith alone in Jesus. (Romans 1:17; James 2:14)

- Mercy and salvation are by faith as much as obedience is by faith. (Romans 1:5; James 2:17)

- The Bible is the inspired Word of God and only through the Holy Spirit may we understand the Word and fellowship with the living God. (2 Timothy 3:16; Luke 24:45)

- It is only through Jesus, God's Son, that a man can be saved. (Acts 4:12)

- He rose from the dead and will return. (1 Thessalonians 4:17–18)

- There is a heaven and a hell. (Revelation 20:10)

- God is one, yet in three persons. (John 14:9)

- Salvation is a gift from God that He works in those being saved who have faith in Jesus. (2 Corinthians 2:15)

- Only those who hate their own lives, pick up a cross and follow Jesus by faith are Christians.
  (John 12:25; Luke 14:25–35; Luke 9:23)

- Only those who "hate and despise" money through faith in Jesus are serving God. (Matthew 6:24)

- Spiritual insanity is not to be allowed in the church.
  (2 Corinthians 11:23)

- We preach a full message of faith, which includes the blood, Spirit and water of Jesus. (Acts 5:20; 1 John 5:6–8)

- Leadership can and should be held accountable by the power of the Holy Spirit. (1 Timothy 5:20; 1 John 1:7)

- The grace of God, received by faith, is the power to obey, not an excuse for sin and disobedience. (Titus 2:11–14)

- We do not think we are the only church. (Luke 9:49–50)

- We do not preach hermeneutics or miracles; we preach the gospel of faith alone in Jesus.
  (1 Corinthians 1:22–23; 2:1)

- Any one not picking up and embracing the offensive message of the cross by faith in Jesus will miss all the doctrine's listed above and true faith in Jesus. (1 Corinthians 2:2; Galatians 5:11)

Appendix

# Salvation by Works

. . . not by works, so that no one can boast. (Ephesians 2:9)

We are not saved by works!" is usually the knee-jerk reaction to any suggestion today that we should actually obey Scripture. We need, however, to stop acting like brute beasts that believe by instinct rather than by enlightened faith.

We must understand one thing very clearly. A person does not become legalistic by obeying Scripture. If that were the case then all the Apostles would have fallen from grace. Indeed, remember that Paul preached obedience—obedience that comes from faith, but obedience nonetheless. The bottom line is that if a man has true faith in Jesus, his life conforming to Scripture testifies of that faith. As a preacher I am to preach obedience, to "call" for an obedience that comes faith.[1]

Through him and for his name's sake, we received grace and apostleship to *call* people from among all the Gentiles to the *obedience that comes from faith.* (Romans 1:5, emphasis added)

Three kinds of "obedience" take place in the church today. Only one, however, is the true obedience that comes from honest belief in Jesus.

- "Spirit-filled" and "charismatic" obedience: The claiming of the Holy Spirit without obedience. Where emotions and the flesh feels elevated to the position of God. It is an emotional, fleshly application of Scripture with each person doing whatever feels comfortable to them.

- Legalistic and logical obedience: Scripture is obeyed selectively, but without surrender to the Holy Spirit and cross. This is true legalism.

- The obedience of true discipleship: Surrender to the Holy Spirit that allows grace to work obedience to Scripture. This is the new life that Jesus came to bring.

Let us look at these points in greater detail.

## True Rebellion

First of all, some believers claim to have the Holy Spirit, but they do not obey Scripture. Such is the case for the vast majority of "Spirit-filled" or "charismatic" Christians. Those on the outside can easily see that such people claim to follow the Word of God, but merely please themselves in the name of Jesus. They are the golden calf worshipers of today that will not wait for the commands of God to flow down from the holy mountain. They desire only to have liberty, fun, and freedom in the name of Jesus. The same thing happened in Exodus 32 when the Israelites made themselves a golden calf and danced around it with great joy and zeal; all in the name of the Lord.

> When Aaron saw this, he built an altar in front of the
> calf and announced, "Tomorrow there will be a festival
> to the Lord." (Exodus 32:5)

Many people say they are filled with the Holy Spirit, yet refuse to obey God. They will often use the tired old excuse that they do not want to be "legalistic" or fall into salvation by works. But simply obeying God's commands does not constitute trying to earn salvation. Nor does doing a work in Christ mean that a man nullifies the free gift of God. Indeed God creates us to do good works that He "prepared in advance for us to do."

> For we are God's workmanship, created in Christ Jesus
> to do good works, which God prepared in advance for
> us to do. (Ephesians 2:10)

If we refuse to allow God to "work" in us, we cut ourselves off from saving grace. A man cannot just do as he pleases, refusing to be moved by God's saving, working grace, and then expect to go to heaven. That would be like the Israelites standing beside the parted Red Sea and whining to God, "This is salvation by works! Why are you asking us to do something? Why do we have to walk across? Why do we have to be baptized in Moses? Why do we have to pass through this water?" If they had stood there with that attitude Pharaoh's army would have destroyed them. Sin and worldliness would have overtaken them. As Jesus would say, "Let the reader understand."

A faith in God unaccompanied by obedience is not a saving faith, but a demonic one that takes selfish liberty in the name of God's mercy. True "friends" of God demonstrate that they receive a true faith, and their actions prove it. For this reason water baptism can save a person without it being a work to earn salvation. For if the Holy Spirit works true faith in a person, there will also be, at the same time, obedience to what God commands. The man or woman who takes the prompting of the Holy Spirit and responds in a manner that God does not command is a rebel and liar. Such a faith cannot save them. If Abraham had tried to offer up a cow instead of his son, he would not have been called a "friend" of God. If a person refuses to obey God's command to be baptized, but instead tries to earn his salvation with a canned prayer, he shouldn't expect to enter heaven.

> Was not our ancestor Abraham considered righteous for what he did when he offered his son Isaac on the altar? You see that his faith and his actions were working together, and his faith was made complete by what he did. And the scripture was fulfilled that says, "Abraham believed God, and it was credited to him as righteousness," and he was called God's friend. (James 2:21–23)

## True Legalism

Secondly, we find the group made up of legalists and "logical" thinkers. They form most of what we consider the mainstream Protestant churches—such as Baptist, church of Christ, Methodist, etc. Though many now embrace the foolishness of the Charismatic type churches, the majority remain very conservative and, in their approach to Scripture, greatly concerned with things like the "historical context" and the Greek or Hebrew. Like the first group, they claim something that they do not really have. They claim a belief in the Holy Spirit, but have no cross to make this a true reality. Such people very logically approach the Scriptures, and base their beliefs on human wisdom, not enlightenment by the Holy Spirit and a mind crucified by Christ.

As we have already seen, it is *how* we obey that determines whether a person has fallen into legalism. The test of legalism is not the number of Scriptures we obey but *how* we obey those Scriptures. Jesus condemned Bible study by human effort when He declared that many people refused to come to Him to have true life. Christians can "diligently study the Scriptures" but refuse to submit to the cross of Jesus, so their Bible studies and debates have no life. They are legalists that seek to obey Scripture apart from the power of Jesus Christ, even as they lay claim to that power.

> You diligently study the Scriptures because you think that by them you possess eternal life. These are the Scriptures that testify about me, yet you refuse to come to me to have life. (John 5:39–40)

If a person seeks to obey by human effort or, in other words, if they try to use their own mind to apply Scripture to their life, they fall under legalism. On the next page is the Scripture that defines legalism. It is trying to apply the Bible to our own life in the best manner we can. Legalism is choosing how we view Scriptures and how we will apply them. It uses our own minds to understand and obey Scripture.

> Are you so foolish? After beginning with the Spirit, are you now trying to attain your goal by human effort? (Galatians 3:3)

Everyone who goes to church obeys some set of rules or principles, which must be crucified. The only kind of obedience that counts is one that comes from death to self by the power of the Holy Spirit.

Legalists and logical thinkers do not want to give up their lives and follow the Holy Spirit in everything, so they turn to outlines, Biblical principals, and their own concepts of what Scripture commands us to obey. This is actually the kind of Christianity most people walk in, even though they may talk about being Spirit-filled. Legalism is merely a man taking some idea out of the Bible and seeking to live it in his own strength and understanding. Salvation by works is nothing less than living by godly principles or getting oneself pumped up from a sermon and setting out to live those principles. It is the Garden of Eden lived out all over again, where each man decides what is right and wrong for himself. This is true salvation by works and in the end it cannot save a person. Fig leaf faith will never cover our sin.

**True Life**

The third and last type of obedience is demonstrated by those who have found the narrow gate and walk the narrow road. They allow the Holy Spirit to crucify human effort in their life and do not rebel against the demands of grace. They understand that God's grace provides the power to live the Christian life. Indeed, they see no excuse for not living it. True humility marks their walk, along with rich obedience.

His divine power has given us everything we need for life and godliness through our knowledge of him who called us by his own glory and goodness. (2 Peter 1:3)

Look above again at what Peter wrote. The kind of faith that comes from heaven is loaded with power to obey. We have no excuse when we fail. We must admit our stubbornness and self-righteousness, for "His divine power has given us everything we need for life and godliness." The church today so easily shouts "legalism" because it overflows with rebels that have no honest desire to obey God by grace. The church claims to know God but, by their actions, prove the opposite and are "unfit for doing anything good."

> They claim to know God, but by their actions they deny him. They are detestable, disobedient and unfit for doing anything good. (Titus 1:16)

If anyone says they have faith in God but does not have a life full of obedience, then they do *not* have a faith that comes from heaven. Instead it is man's faith, man's opinion, man's religion, and man's idea of the Bible. That kind of faith is man working to follow Jesus—it is salvation by works.

God only gives the Holy Spirit to those who "obey him." Obey "*Him*," and not our idea of what Scripture says or what a denomination declares. Those unwilling to submit to God's commands by saving grace simply do not have the Holy Spirit.

> We are witnesses of these things, and so is the Holy Spirit, whom God has given to those who obey him. (Acts 5:32)

Only those who are willing to listen to the voice of the Holy Spirit leading and instructing them daily, will find the New Life. All others are liars, thieves, and robbers trying to earn their salvation in some other way.

**True Saving Faith**

Can faith without deeds save a man?

Can faith without . . .

    . . . denying self
    . . . taking the Lord's Supper
    . . . hearing God's voice
    . . . baptism
    . . . hating one's own life
    . . . despising the dollar
    . . . prayer
    . . . going to church
    . . . taking proper roles in church
    . . . watching what we watch
    . . . giving to the poor
    . . . watching what we say
    . . . being led by the Spirit
    . . . hating our father, mother, brother and sisters
    . . . giving up all
    . . . hair length that glorifies God
    . . . becoming aliens and strangers in the world
    . . . and all the many other Scriptures save a man or
        woman?

God, through James, has already given us the answer.

What good is it, my brothers, if a man claims to have faith
but has no deeds? Can such faith save him? (James 2:14)

So, finally, what is salvation by works? What is legalism? Simply, man trying to obey anything apart from the
guidance and empowerment of the Holy Spirit. It is not the
fact that a man obeys God's commands in Scripture. To only

claim that we are saved by faith, as currently understood by the church, is to deliberately ignore the Bible and rebel against how God defines His grace. Such belief rebels against God's actual grace and mercy. What a heavy judgment will befall such individuals for they have trampled on the blood of Jesus they claim so strongly to have faith in. After all, mercy gives man time to repent, act, obey, and listen to the voice of the Holy Spirit. Let us not sin against heaven itself by misunderstanding mercy.

> The Lord is not slow in keeping his promise, as some understand slowness. He is patient with you, not wanting anyone to perish, but everyone to come to repentance. (2 Peter 3:9)

Let me recap again what we have covered, because those who hold to once saved always saved will inevitably try to confuse the issue. We are *not* saved by our works. Every true Christian can agree with Paul that works do not save us. We all agree that salvation is a free gift from God.

Most people have never really thought about the true meaning of "salvation by works." They may have some vague ideas about trying to earn their salvation, but they rarely turn to Scripture for a true definition. The most common current understanding usually boils down to this: if you teach that a person has to "do" anything in order to be saved, then you preach salvation by works. We have already seen the blatant hypocrisy of such a statement. Even teaching that we just have to ask Jesus into our hearts still advocates that we "do" something.

We must accept on Jesus' terms an understanding of what it means to trust Him for salvation, not what we wish He meant. "Trust" has come to mean just a shallow verbal acknowledgment that Jesus died for our sins. Nowhere in

Scripture will we find such a concept. Even the demons[2] know that. To trust or have faith in Jesus means that we obey Him by the power of the Holy Spirit as the cross is allowed to crucify self. To sum up our choices in the Lord:

- Holy Spirit without Obedience = Rebellion
- Obedience without the Holy Spirit = Legalism
- Holy Spirit with Obedience = The New Life

Which choice will you make?

# Endnotes

**Chapter 1: Jesus Spoke Clearly**
1. Luke 14:32
2. Luke 6:48
3. 2 Corinthians 4:10
4. Luke 12:21, Colossians 1:10
5. 2 Corinthians 13:5
6. Jeremiah 2:23–25
7. Revelation 3:1

**Chapter 2: How Fruit Turns Bad**
1. 1 Corinthians 4:20
2. John 15:8
3. Acts 23:8

**Chapter 3: True Salvation**
1. John 15:8
2. Acts 20:19
3. Luke 14:28, 31
4. Psalm 51:5
5. Hebrews 3:17
6. 1 Peter 3:21

7. Romans 1:17
8. Titus 2:11–12
9. If a man refused the blood of Jesus or the Holy Spirit individuals would declare he was not saved. Few would think of leaving out the blood and the Holy Spirit, but show no holy fear in leaving out the water. Yet, John tells us the three are in agreement, of equal importance and power, see 1 John 5:8. This is often why when baptism is mentioned in Scripture it doesn't say the word water baptism. Because it is a baptism of the Spirit, the blood, and water. It is all one baptism which reflects not only the triune nature of God, but that when God saves a man He does so completely.
10. Mark 1:14–15

## Chapter 4: Falling Away

1. Psalm 2:12
2. Acts 9:31
3. 2 Corinthians 7:11
4. 1 John 3:15; Hebrews 12:16
5. Jeremiah 17:9
6. Hebrews 12:14–15
7. Galatians 5:25
8. Luke 13:7
9. Titus 2:12
10. 1 Corinthians 11:14–15
11. Titus 2:11–13
12. Romans 6:14
13. 1 John 3:9
14. 1 John 5:16
15. John 7:24
16. James 5:16
17. Matthew 28:19
18. 1 Timothy 2:4
19. John 6:61–69

## Chapter 5: Living Like This

1. Romans 10:10; 2 Corinthians 2:15; 1 Peter 1:5; 1 Corinthians 1:18; Ephesians 2:5; Philippians 1:28; 2 Timothy 1:9; Hebrews 9:28; 1 Thessalonians 5:8; Romans 8:24; Ephesians 1:13–14; Romans 13:11; Ephesians 1:4–5

2. 1 Corinthians 15:34–53; Colossians 3:3
3. 1 Corinthians 9:27
4. Philippians 2:12
5. Acts 26:14
6. Ezekiel 13:10
7. John 10:1
8. Matthew 28:18–20
9. John 12:24
10. Luke 14:25–35; Luke 16:13
11. *The Essential Piece,* by Timothy Williams, ISBN 1-57921-293-X
12. Luke 19:17

## Chapter 6: Thorn Bushes and Briers

1. *Even the Demons Believe,* by Timothy Williams,
   ISBN 1-57921-355-3
2. *Insanity in the Church,* by Timothy Williams, ISBN 1-57921-390-1
3. Acts 2:38
4. Luke 14:28, 31
5. Daniel 11:34
6. 1 Corinthians 4:21; 1 Timothy 1:3
7. 1 Corinthians 13:1

## Chapter 7: The Solution

1. John 6:45
2. Jeremiah 4:3; Hosea 10:12; Matthew 15:14

## Chapter 8: The Fearful Estate of Francis Spira

1. See Chapter 9
2. James 1:12 (emphasis added)
3. 2 Timothy 2:5

## Chapter 9: If You Think You Are Falling Away

1. There are men, like the fig tree Jesus cursed, whose withering happens in a moment or instance, whose chance of repentance is gone in a matter of seconds and for all practical purposes never are given another chance. See Mark 11:20–21; 8:24
2. Matthew 12:20

3. The believer in once saved always saved knows nothing about the pain of being born again, for to be born again is just a simple matter of mocking a prayer. They do not understand the work and labor that goes before, during, and after a man is born again.
4. Luke 13:24
5. 1 John 1:7
6. Colossians 1:29

## Who Is Timothy Williams?
1. Acts 4:13

## Appendix: Salvation by Works
1. Faith is not that we hear faith's call, then act or don't act as we think best. Rather faith calls, faith guides, faith empowers, and faith acts. Anything less is the pride of religious man.
2. *Even the Demons Believe,* by Timothy Williams, ISBN 1-57921-355-3

# Other Books by Timothy Williams

**Even the Demons Believe**
- A small book that details how to get started in the new life of Christ.
  ISBN: 1-57921-355-3

**Insanity in the Church**
- Exposes the errors of loving self that are in the church and introduces the solution.
  ISBN: 1-57921-390-1

**Whisper Revival**
- How to prepare yourself for revival when God moves, as well as what dangers to look for.
  ISBN: 1-57921-274-3

## 101 Ways to Deny Self
- This book is based on 1 Peter 1:13 where we are called to prepare our minds for action. It is not a list of rules, but a preparation for the Holy Spirit to guide us in joyful obedience.
  ISBN: 1-57921-397-9

## The Essential Piece
- A very hard hitting, detailed book about the offensive message of the cross. It is a difficult read and one will have to persevere to get through it. If the reader does, rich joy will be found.
  ISBN: 1-57921-293-X

## eau de Cult
- This book explains the fruit of God's love being worked in a body of believers and how many will consider that to look like a cult.
  ISBN 1-57921-511-4

## Bewitchment – The Foolish Galatians
- While this book is written to a specific denomination it really is a call to all of us to be sure we are walking in the Spirit and not human effort.
  ISBN: 1-57921-469-X

## Prosperity Teachers
- This book reveals how and when God gives us the desires of our hearts. it will cause you to carefully examine what the Bible teaches on prosperity
  ISBN 1-57921-489-4

To order additional copies of

# BAD FRUIT
## THE RESULT OF ONCE SAVED ALWAYS SAVED

call

**Toll free: (877) 421-READ (7323)**

Printed in the United States
33643LVS00002B/106